Declutter Your Mind

Effective Strategies to Free Yourself From Anxiety and Worry

(Easy Steps to Follow to Pave Your Way to Success and Simplifying Life for a Happier)

William Nadeau

Published By **Phil Dawson**

William Nadeau

All Rights Reserved

Declutter Your Mind: Effective Strategies to Free Yourself From Anxiety and Worry (Easy Steps to Follow to Pave Your Way to Success and Simplifying Life for a Happier)

ISBN 978-1-7388580-3-3

No part of this guidebook shall be reproduced in any form without permission in writing from the publisher except in the case of brief quotations embodied in critical articles or reviews.

Legal & Disclaimer

The information contained in this book is not designed to replace or take the place of any form of medicine or professional medical advice. The information in this book has been provided for educational & entertainment purposes only.

The information contained in this book has been compiled from sources deemed reliable, and it is accurate to the best of the Author's knowledge; however, the Author cannot guarantee its accuracy and validity and cannot be held liable for any errors or omissions. Changes are periodically made to this book. You must consult your doctor or get professional medical advice before using any of the suggested remedies, techniques, or information in this book.

Upon using the information contained in this book, you agree to hold harmless the Author from and against any damages, costs, and expenses, including any legal fees potentially resulting from the application of any of the information provided by this guide. This disclaimer applies to any damages or injury caused by the use and application, whether directly or indirectly, of any advice or information presented, whether for breach of contract, tort, negligence, personal injury, criminal intent, or under any other cause of action.

You agree to accept all risks of using the information presented inside this book. You need to consult a professional medical practitioner in order to ensure you are both able and healthy enough to participate in this program.

Table Of Contents

Chapter 1: The Four Different Types Of Stress 1

Chapter 2: The Effect Of Stress On Health 9

Chapter 3: The Best Way To Deal With Negative Emotions 13

Chapter 4: 23 Quick Things To Do When You Are Stressed Out 16

Chapter 5: 8 Effective Anger Management Techniques 71

Chapter 6: 20 Magical Steps To Happiness 76

Chapter 7: 6 Secrets To Become Happier 90

Chapter 8: Causes Of Stress 97

Chapter 9: How Stress Affects You 101

Chapter 10: Why Fix Stress 109

Chapter 11: Fixing Stress The Minimalist Way 115

Chapter 12: Set Priorities 129

Chapter 13: Develop A Routine 139

Chapter 14: Journaling 150

Chapter 15: Allow Time To Reflect 158

Chapter 16: Let Go Of The Past 167

Chapter 17: Schedule A Digital Break ... 177

Chapter 1: The Four Different Types of Stress

Everyone talks about stress. Many people may say that they are harassed. In college, I regularly listen this at some stage in tests and time limits.

When we are burdened, possibilities are we have a tendency to find out an answer. And regularly, we are seeking advice from the internet hoping to locate immediately comfort. However, pressure manipulate may not be clean. It contradicts to what maximum people would possibly undergo in thoughts.

The cause in the returned of is that there are actually one in every of a kind varieties of strain. And each kind has a effective diploma or degree of tendencies, symptoms and signs and signs and symptoms, and length. Thus, awesome remedy strategies are desired.

Here are the kinds of stress.

1. Acute strain

Have you professional being unprepared to take the exam or the system interview of a major business enterprise? Chances are you skilled acute stress.

Acute stress is a commonplace pressure that we enjoy each day. It is an instantaneous end result of our each day lives' name for that we want to meet.

Acute strain is thrilling on the equal time because the perceived danger is small. In truth, a little pressure is tough. For instance, reporting in the front of the elegance is every traumatic and tough regardless of the truth that you realize you can cope with it.

But an excessive amount of of acute stress is hard. For instance, cramming for tests at the same time beating the reduce-off date for your obligations may be too much at the manner to address. In this situation, the strain can purpose a extra tough intellectual trouble.

However, in most instances, acute strain is possible. And maximum people appear to have accustomed to this type of pressure. We learn how to regulate and count on viable conditions.

For example, a scholar can also discover ways to avoid cramming by using way of manner of studying and making his/her tasks early. A task applicant may additionally moreover prepare himself for the approaching interview earlier to advantage self-self assurance.

In every examples, acute strain is achievable. The pinnacle hassle about acute pressure is that we excellent revel in it in a short term. And because of the truth it's miles short-term it does no longer have any big horrific impact at the frame. Nonetheless, it has severa signs.

First, a pressured individual also can experience emotional misery. S/he can be irritated, irritable, disturbing and depressed.

Secondly, someone may additionally moreover revel in a few bodily ache along with a headache, again ache, muscular tensions, and jaw ache.

Thirdly, the expanded blood pressure, heartbeat, coronary coronary coronary heart palpitations, dizziness, bloodless and sweaty hands, scarcity of breath and chest pain may be skilled.

2. Episodic acute strain

Episodic acute strain is one of the types of stress this is observed amongst humans who have a distressful lifestyles. This form of pressure is just like the primary elegance. Only that is greater commonplace than the latter.

People who be laid low with the use of episodic acute pressure will be predisposed to be dashing all of the time but they continuously fail to conquer the deadline. They moreover generally will be inclined to take the whole lot awesome to find out they can't take care of it.

If untreated, episodic strain can extensively have an impact on one's capabilities and each day functioning. S/he can also find issues at artwork and in his/her dating.

People who're struggling episodic acute stress also have physical troubles together with migraines, excessive blood stress, complications and chest pains.

They will be inclined to be detrimental to others that may bring about relationship deterioration and another shape of false impression.

Like treating specific kinds of pressure, handling episodic acute stress might also additionally comprise the care of experts. And the remedy manner may additionally additionally remaining for months or so.

However, the remedy may be hard. People with this shape of strain are reluctant to go through trade. They don't forget that there's not whatever wrong with them. The satisfactory difficulty that continues them within the remedy approach is their purpose of treating their pain and soreness.

3. Chronic strain

Chronic strain is some other shape of stress that often reasons the character a burn-out. People who have this shape of stress may also additionally experience being restrained in a awful scenario with out a opportunity of breaking out. Such notion leads them to continual melancholy.

There are many reasons why an man or woman experience this stress. Most of the time, the principle causes are fitness troubles, alcohol consuming, unhappy marriage, violence, and discriminations.

However, some reasons of persistent strain incorporate poor early life critiques. It can be maltreatment, toddler abuse, and precise stressful occasions that someone can also additionally though stay in.

Chronic strain can kill. Many sufferers ended up killing themselves. The not unusual consequences are suicide, stroke, coronary heart attack, violence, and sometimes most cancers.

Chronic strain moreover may be hard to cope with. It calls for the help of professionals. The commonplace remedy is the mixture of clinical, behavioral, and pressure control.

four. Post-disturbing Stress Disorder (PTSD)

Post-disturbing stress ailment is a pressure due to any horrifying or disturbing sports activities. The common evaluations can be formative years maltreatment, poverty, violence, wars, and so forth.

The positioned up-traumatic illness is often determined amongst squaddies who've previous war reviews and with folks that experienced catastrophic activities. For example, after the September 11 assault, more Americans had been diagnosed with PTSD.

People who've PTSD may experience flashbacks of the disturbing occasion which motives trouble in napping. Furthermore, humans with PTSD might also moreover moreover enjoy guilt, despair, emotional indifference, and fear.

Like specific styles of pressure, PTSD have to have a horrible effect on one's each day functioning. A man or woman can't be effective in the place of business due to the winning signs. In fact, in a few instances, people with PTSD have problems with their intimate courting and social connection.

Stress isn't always continually awful. It can, every so often, make us effective. However, people have special responses to stressful activities. Thus, the symptoms and symptoms may be one-of-a-kind from one person to every unique.

One of the quality processes to stay away from strain is to stay energetic and feature higher social connections. Many studies placed that social interactions can make us happy.

However, while you revel in bodily symptoms and signs of any styles of strain which includes headaches, muscle, insomnia, and again pain, find out professional assist.

Stress may be a burden if you do no longer percent it with others. People who have horrible social connection discover it hard to get over depression. While people who talk with their loved ones extra often have higher emotional and highbrow health.

Chapter 2: The Effect of Stress on Health

Psychological stress is part of anyone's every day life. Stress is in maximum cases because of work, poverty, marital issues and distinctive lifestyles's sports. If not resolved, mental stress will bring about denser highbrow troubles.

Psychological strain has been related to numerous bodily and psychological issues. Recent research positioned increasingly more evidence which suggest that stress has terrible influences on nearly all additives of the body.

For instance, one observe tested whether or not or not the perceived horrible health impact of strain is related to coronary heart illness.

The information come to be drawn from 7268 people. For eighteen years of observation, the result shows that 352 deaths associated with coronary coronary coronary heart sickness or professional myocardial infarction (MI) incidents were attributed to the awful perception of pressure.

Participants who perceived that strain can reason a horrible effect on their fitness were two times much more likely to go through coronary heart-related ailments than folks who don't don't forget that stress has a horrible effect on their health.

Meaning whilst you take delivery of as real with that stress can negatively have an effect on your health, you will be more likely to suffer coronary coronary heart ailment than specific people. Another take a look at additionally decided that intellectual pressure is a hazard detail for cardiovascular illnesses.

The most modern-day posted observe on The Lancet strengthens the preceding findings. Emotional stress is determined to have an association with cardiovascular ailment.

The cited link between mental pressure and cardiovascular disorder modified into due to amygdala hobby. Amygdala is a small place of the mind this is answerable for generating human feelings which incorporates anger, worry, unhappiness, in addition to controlling aggressive conduct.

The examine similarly shows that:

"Amygdalar interest is involved in part via a route that includes improved bone-marrow hobby and arterial contamination. These findings provide novel insights into the mechanism through which emotional stressors can lead to cardiovascular contamination in humans."

But despite the fact that those pieces of evidence provide a brand new manner of further records stress, it have to be interpreted with warning.

In the technical or statistical factor of view, most studies on mental pressure had been correlational in nature (best looking for hyperlinks amongst variables). Hence, no "motive and effect" became installed.

Although stress is associated with cardiovascular illness, it ought to not be interpreted as strain is the inflicting trouble of cardiovascular sickness.

It might be that stress is the purpose of CVD, but for now, as regular with the evidence shows, we can not offer a solid give up. We can simplest companion strain with CVD.

But previous studies are beneficial sufficient to lighten the arena. I preference that in the near future extra physiological studies could be carried out to offer hard proof in this do not forget.

Chapter 3: The Best Way to Deal with Negative Emotions

Most humans while they will be feeling awful make impulsive selections. The trouble is that the selections you're making whilst you're indignant regularly result in bad results. So what's the wonderful trouble to do at the same time as you're angry?

Instead of giving an answer based on rationalization, I will provide you with a scientifically confirmed manner to effectively address horrific emotions. A test published in 2017 determined that accepting your bad feeling is the extraordinary manner to address it.

It is ironic due to the truth humans who've been able to sense horrible feelings have been sincerely happier than folks who deny their emotion.

In addition, feeling your negative feelings may additionally make you glad due to the fact the take a look at indicates.

The first author of the have a study, Dr. Maya Tamir concluded:

"Happiness is extra than without a doubt feeling delight and keeping off pain. Happiness is about having critiques that are tremendous and treasured, which incorporates feelings which you count on are the proper ones to have.

All emotions may be excessive notable in some contexts and bad in others, regardless of whether or not or not they may be quality or unpleasant."

Most people hate terrible emotions. That's why they react after they revel in or experience the upcoming unhappy occasion. However, avoidance isn't the quality manner to deal with horrible emotions. It is understanding and reputation. Understand what it's miles that you are feeling. Are you annoyed, indignant, or agitated?

The next detail to do is accepting your right emotion. Do now not deny it. Breath. Get a few glowing air. This will permit you to loosen up.

Smile and exchange your internal conversation. Instead of telling your self which you're dissatisfied, trade the terms. Make them wonderful.

Do now not located blame on others. No don't forget how bad you revel in, do now not issue palms. Take responsibility. The most effective person who's liable for your lifestyles and very very own feeling is you. Don't waste some time on self-pity and remorse. Accept what has passed off and go together with the go with the flow on.

Chapter 4: 23 Quick Things to Do When You Are Stressed Out

It can be unexpected to apprehend that strain is simply contagious. A new medical proof has hooked up it. Although the researchers used animals because the difficulty of the test, the locating is extensive. Meaning, it can be real to human beings too. In the latter have a look at, the authors stated that a person else's pressure can be transmitted or obtained.

Professor Jaideep Bains, the leading author of the examine shared his forestall. "Recent research endorse that strain and emotions may be 'contagious," Bains said. "Whether this has lasting results for the mind is not seemed."

The implication of the research may be massive to anybody. It might also moreover moreover advise that paying attention to a pressured character might also have a negative impact in your mental properly-being.

It might be that listening to unhappy tales can also want to make you pressured out. Or, you could have already made your friend pressured once you shared your bad revel in.

Professor Bains is aware of this opportunity. "We certainly speak our pressure to others, once in a while with out even expertise it," Bains brought. "There is even evidence that some signs of pressure can persist in family and cherished ones of individuals who be afflicted by PTSD." What are you capable of do if you already confused out? Can you zap the pressure away?

There can be no unmarried method to the ones questions. But there are various techniques you can use to ease your intellectual pressure.

1. Stop ingesting too much caffeine, tobacco, and alcohol

Avoid consuming caffeinated drinks, nicotine, and alcohol. These materials are stimulants. This manner that the ones materials need to increase your pressure level.

The awesome trouble you could do rather is ingesting some of water, herbal teas, and fruit juices. Fruits have natural dietary contents that assist enhance your bodily and intellectual fitness.

2. Stay energetic

Many subjects ought to make you compelled out. It may be your day hobby, your dating, monetary troubles, and so forth. If you keep in mind you studied you reached the breaking point, prevent. Just take a walk and get sparkling air. If you may, visit the fitness center. Physical sports are beneficial to loosen up your frame and mind. If you lighten up your mind, you are recuperation not simplest your highbrow fitness however additionally your complete frame.

Every time you understand threat, your body responds. The thoughts sends a message to the adrenal gland to launch a hormone referred to as adrenaline.

The adrenal gland is an endocrine gland due to this that the chemical it releases will circulate in the bloodstream. The launched adrenaline will then be part of the blood float which in turn will increase the sugar within the blood, will growth heartbeat, and blood strain.

Then the hypothalamus, a mind's vicinity, will deliver a signal to the pituitary gland. This gland will launch factors in an effort to stimulate the adrenal cortex in an effort to result in cortisol secretion. Cortisol is a strain hormone. It allows the body to generate greater electricity enough to escape the dangerous scenario.

However, the extended amount of cortisol inside the blood glide will negatively have an effect on the immune device. Furthermore, it could also harm the thoughts cells that may result in reminiscence impairment. In fact, in plenty of instances, long-term strain can also motive stroke and coronary coronary heart attack.

The pressure and thoughts

Studies within the past many years advocate that stress may additionally additionally damage the thoughts. Too masses amount of cortisol will harm the cells within the hippocampus area this is answerable for reminiscence garage. In addition, severa research determined that continual stress can reason untimely ageing of the mind cells.

The strain hormone cortisol is essential on your survival. But too much of it's far in reality dangerous. Chronic strain will even bring about melancholy and one-of-a-kind highbrow issues.

So how can you shield your brain from strain?

Relieving pressure regularly consists of treatment. But a trendy examine decided a totally smooth way to deal with stress free of rate. The researchers positioned that jogging may be pretty beneficial in kicking out the strain. In truth, the check shows that strolling facilitates contrary the effect of pressure on mind cells.

The foremost author, Dr. Jeff Edwards described the give up end result. "Exercise is a simple and price-effective way to eliminate the terrible influences on the memory of continual stress," Edwards said. You can maximize learning if you are stress-loose. The utility of this surrender result may be huge for each academic and real-life conditions.

To control your stress and mind well, you need to discover time to carry out a simple bodily interest which consist of jogging. This is the most effective exercise that enables you stay psychologically and mentally healthful.

"It's empowering to comprehend that we can combat the horrible affects of strain on our brains absolutely via manner of getting out and taking walks," Edwards delivered.

3. Get sufficient sleep

Only currently, researchers determined that loss of sleep is a giant motive of depression. Not exceptional that, sleep deprivation additionally deteriorates cognitive functioning. This technique that during case you're pressured out or depressed, you received't be capable of function commonly. You can't suppose and perform properly to your every day everyday.

The key to getting sufficient sleep is making your thoughts comfortable earlier than going to bed. Forget the responsibilities that you need to have finished on a sure day. Detach yourself from terrible mind. Everything has its proper time. Do now not add your destiny problem to your present problem.

And ultimately, restriction your show time. In other phrases, do not use your mobile telephones and special gadgets earlier than bed. Studies show that the mild that emanates from the display of your gadgets will prevent your sleepiness.

four. Try relaxing sports

If you can, attempt meditation. Several research had hooked up its effectiveness in gaining intellectual calmness. Meditation is a thousand-365 days-antique practice. However, high-quality in contemporary years that technological know-how commenced out to recognize its usefulness. If you could get rid of your worries, you will be capable of calm your thoughts.

five. Speak out your hassle

Needless to mention that issues compelled you out. If you trust you studied you can't cope with the trouble or find it hard to treatment, it's miles a splendid concept to find a few assist. You can ask your pals, your co-personnel, loved ones, or maybe expert specialists whom you accept as true with you studied may additionally want to provide you a solution.

A tension that has no outlet will become a greater excessive highbrow hassle. Depression, for instance, emanates from a simple pressure.

Stress is not best the motive of intellectual issues however moreover bodily contamination. Studies had installed that stomach ulcer is attributable to intellectual stress. So remove stress in advance than it harms you.

6. Focus on the answer of the problem

Many humans become even extra careworn out because of the reality they recognition at the problem with out figuring out possible solutions.

Once you turn out to be aware about the trouble, the following step you need to do is locating the manner out. Do no longer are residing at the depth of the hassle. It is given. Control your emotion.

Nothing will occur in case you allow yourself be completed with the useful resource of the ache. Use your mind. Think and don't allow your bad emotions cloud your hobby. Once you decided the manner out, act on it. It's the powerful manner to kick out pressure.

7. Use it slow wisely

Stress will begin to kick in whilst you have a propensity to attention on many stuff concurrently. I constantly see this among university university college college students. They great make their tasks or write their time period papers at the same time as cut-off dates are speedy drawing near.

But that is a lousy exercise. Why? Because your mind can't attend to many stimuli in a given time. It isn't always designed to attain this. The greater you cram, the more you are making errors, and the extra you turn out to be burdened out. Time manage may be very critical. Make a list of the things you want to do on day after today. And live in your agenda.

8. Learn to disagree

One of the motives of stress is social strain. You need to comply to the group to healthy in. But doing this may sabotage your loose will. When you stress your self to behave like others do, you're faking yourself. This, in flip creates cognitive dissonance so that you can, of direction, result in pressure.

The pleasant problem you can do rather is following your non-public will. Be indifferent to what others might be wondering. As lengthy as you do not harm everybody, you'll be good enough.

9. Take a relaxation

You aren't a device or a robot. Your frame desires relaxation. Physical fatigue may even bring about highbrow fatigue. So in case you are worn-out at art work, find time for a rest. If you could, take a vacation. Visit lovable sceneries. Leave all of the traumatic topics in the again of. In this way, you'll be capable of rest your mind.

We are dwelling in a very worrying global. Either in art work or at college, we are continuously chasing chores. We continually beat closing dates. As a quit result, taking a ruin can be the least choice.

Michael Guttridge, a place of business conduct psychologist says that "There's an idea we must usually be available, artwork all of the time. It's hard to interrupt out of that and visit the park."

However, the obvious surrender give up end result of being busy is the tendency of turning into detached to precise essential topics. Parents, as an instance, may forget about about their obligations to their little children, and good sized others.

"People consume on the desk and get food at the laptop — it's disgusting. They want to transport for a stroll, to the espresso store, absolutely get away. Even Victorian factories had a few shape of rest breaks," Guttridge brought.

The truth is, taking a destroy is beneficial to our mental functioning. In truth, it's miles important. Wasting time is what we want to refresh our thoughts and frame. Guttridge believes that taking some time to relaxation is in fact healthful. "Wasting time is ready recharging your battery and de-cluttering," he stated.

The Chinese humans have a pronouncing this is going: "Too a incredible deal of a first rate stuff is a awful stuff." This is in truth right. Even Henry Ford understood the importance of giving a person a destroy. Thus he started out the eight-hour every day ordinary.

Henry Ford best required his employees to art work 8 hours an afternoon, five days in keeping with week. He gave them days to relaxation (Saturday and Sunday). Ford determined that his employees have turn out to be extra inexperienced and green at the meeting line.

Resting lets in our body to regain energy. Scientific research found that taking a damage boosts attention and productivity.

Of path, we want to grind and push ourselves to finish a given task. But it should no longer save you us from taking a smash. Sometimes we need to lie low from artwork although it sounds "dropping time".

10. Listen to track

It is incredible to realise how tune have to ease a involved thoughts. Several research had placed that a soothing track has a splendid exquisite effect on human emotion.

The extremely good tune sorts that would with out trouble zap strain are the instrumentals. Why? Because songs with lyrics strain the thoughts to make an interpretation. As a give up quit result, the mind will no longer be capable of loosen up.

Managing pressure can be a undertaking. Most humans are caught in a demanding condition due to the truth they don't recognize the manner to manipulate it. But with the non-save you attempt of technological information, solutions grow to be to be had. You don't want to buy medication for any form of stress.

For instance, a present day day have a look at decided the current day way to put off stress proper away. This approach is short and clean. All you want is a pen and a piece of paper. Music remedy have become determined to be powerful in lowering despair amongst younger humans. It additionally boosts conceitedness. The end come to be primarily based at the previous take a look at of greater than hundred individuals.

The researchers divided the members into agencies. One institution underwent tune treatment on the equal time due to the fact the alternative served as a manipulate enterprise. During the test, the researchers requested the humans' emotions as they play a certain music.

The result determined that the people who have been given the remedy had higher self-esteem and decrease depression stage. This have a test may be very beneficial in treating younger human beings with behavioral problems. It also can manual specialists in making appropriate movements. The lead author of the observe, Professor Sam Porter gave his wonderful end.

"The findings contained in our report have to be considered by using healthcare organizations and commissioners whilst making selections approximately the kind of cope with more youthful humans that they want to guide," stated Porter.

Music treatment has been spherical for 1000 of years. In truth, ancient Greek philosophers used track for treatment. Depressed human beings were informed to be aware of calming music of a flute. However, within the current-day time, the formal tune treatment practices started out out in 1940's. After the Second World War, intellectual health experts used tune remedy on squaddies with PTSD.

Musicians visit highbrow institutions to play tune for infantrymen who had trauma. Since then medical professionals started out to understand the usefulness of track remedy.

We all have every day testimonies that make us compelled out. It might be your boss at work, your college assignments, or your love existence. No consider how we strive to keep away from terrible sports, unwanted evaluations seem now not viable to persuade clear of.

Thus, at the same time as pressure moves, we typically usually have a tendency to find out answers. The internet is the richest supply of statistics almost about curing emotional burden. You can discover loads of tips and techniques to lessen anxiety.

However, not all of those recommendations are loose and technological understanding-based. In this a part of the ebook, however, I can be going to percentage with you one of the captivating results of clinical research. Without a doubt, this can be a outstanding assist for anybody who wants to loosen up. This stress-reducing method is free and does not need time and area to carry out.

The trick that I'm talking about is a specific track. A music that reduces anxiety as lots as sixty five percent whilst you pay attention to it. It is known as "Weightless", with the aid of Marconi Union.

Dr. David Lewis-Hodgson of Mindlab International has performed a studies to investigate songs that can make humans loosen up.

The people of the check had been advocated to remedy puzzles. The cause of the assignment have become to bring about a nice degree of pressure. While doing the challenge, the people have been moreover being attentive to unique songs due to the fact the researchers measured their physiological states which includes heartbeat blood pressure, and breathing. The finding indicates that paying attention to one music "Weightless" reduces anxiety thru sixty five percentage.

The song "Weightless" become deliberately created by means of Marconi Union with the collaborative attempt of numerous sound therapists. The concord, rhythms, and bass have been cautiously calibrated to make the listeners cushty.

The preceding have a look at is an evidence that music is a wonderful help to human's fitness. This can be the purpose why, at some stage in records, our ancestors had been tune fanatics. Music made them glad and healthful.

The locating is likewise a excellent indication that we can be relaxed with out doing some aspect. By taking note of this shape of tune, we will gain an tension and stress-free mind. The song "weightless" is so powerful that Dr. David Lewis-Hodgson has one warning:

"'Weightless' became so powerful, many ladies have become drowsy and I might also need to recommend in competition to riding while paying attention to the track due to the fact it can be volatile."

How does song treatment reduce depression?

The remedy addresses someone's bodily, emotional and social desires. Creating and paying attention to a track permits people to particular their inner worldwide without actually talking about it. The combination of melody, rhythm, and melody ought to sluggish a person's coronary coronary heart fee, breath, and different physical hobby. The approach triggers the secretion of greater dopamine within the thoughts which in turn boosts happiness.

11. What will you do? Write your feelings down

The previous finding suggests that disclosing your emotion on a piece of a paper allows your mind gain overall performance. This method allows the mind to be unfastened from issues. When you're demanding lots, your brain becomes preoccupied.

When that takes place, you'll find it tough to pay interest. Why? Because your thoughts is doing numerous duties at a time – tracking and suppressing the issues. Hans Schroder, the primary writer of the have a have a look at concluded:

"Our findings show that if you get those worries from your head via expressive writing, the ones cognitive resources are freed up to paintings towards the undertaking you're finishing and you grow to be greater inexperienced."

In exceptional terms, writing down your emotions helps your thoughts benefit consciousness. Expressive writing will not only put off pressure proper away however additionally permits the mind if you want to pay attention at some stage in a demanding challenge.

Another co-author of the observe believes that expressive writing may even help the body to prepare for any upcoming demanding task. Dr. Jason Moser, one of the co-authors of the examine shared his very personal end:

"Expressive writing makes the mind art work lots less hard on upcoming traumatic obligations, that's what worriers often get "burned out" over, their concerned minds operating tougher and warmer."

If you're a person who troubles masses, possibly you need to strive expressive writing. Take a brief time to put in writing down what you experience in the endorse time. It is captivating to understand how smooth to cast off stress immediately. The precise issue about this technique is that it's far brief and easy. 12. Meditate

Our mind wanders. Not quality that, it's far able to perceiving conditions in advance of time. But there's most effective one hassle, occasionally, it exaggerates. Exaggerated mind emerge as fears and problems which in flip result in anxiety.

If the trouble isn't dealt with properly, extra devastating mental issues also can furthermore get up. For a long term, clinical studies in mental disciplines attempt to discover answers. And more regularly than no longer, specialists depend carefully on treatment and remedy to tame a thoughts.

Fortunately, you don't need treatment and highly-priced expert services to fight your worries and anxieties. A new observe determined a easy and loose way to tame a thoughts. A ten-minute mindfulness can be drastically beneficial for annoying people.

A clean mindfulness workout will forestall the thoughts from producing beside the factor thoughts. It additionally enables the mind to gain recognition at the triumphing experience. The predominant creator of the check, Mengran Xu defined the end result. "We also located that meditation practice appears to assist worrying human beings to shift their hobby from their very very very own internal troubles to the existing-second outside global, which lets in higher cognizance on a venture handy," stated Xu.

Mindfulness is not a cutting-edge healing method to ease concerns and anxieties. The historic human beings already exploited its energy numerous thousand years in the beyond.

Only currently, scientists have placed the notable first rate impact of this approach on human's health. The accurate aspect about this exercise is that it's far pretty simple and you can do it in truth anywhere.

Meditation Guide: How to Meditate at Home?

Meditation undeniably has numerous excessive high-quality influences on fitness. It reduces, strain, melancholy and unique highbrow issues. But the manner requires a top notch location. And that first-rate vicinity can be your house. Yes, you may meditate even in with out going out of doors.

Here are the eight steps you can observe to correctly meditate.

1. Find a silent location.

Meditation calls for a quiet vicinity. A location in which you may pay attention. It might be your room, your garage, or maybe in your basement. Any vicinity this is loose from noise.

2. Sit along side your legs crossed on the floor.

Probably you've got seen human beings doing meditation in advance than. They have one commonplace body function - sitting with their legs crossed at the ground. Do the identical way.

3. Sit tall.

Sit immediately and quietly. Imagine which you are leaning on a flat wall.

four. Relax your body.

Close your eyes and begin feeling your body. Maybe you need to start at your feet, ankles up to your head. While doing this, you want to make it tremendous which you are amusing your complete body. Let move of muscle tensions out of your neck, tongue, and shoulders.

5. Be however.

Now that you are comfortable, start paying attention to the sound round you. Just be aware of your surroundings. But do now not react, in reality pay attention quietly. Do now not permit your mind to make any interpretation or analysis at the sound you pay attention. Just be conscious.

6. Breathe deeply.

The next step of doing meditation is to awareness to your respiration. Breathe quietly however deeply. Fill your lungs with air without strain. Feel the sensation because the air passes you nose, throat, and chest at the identical time as doing the whole inhale and exhale technique.

7. Determine while to give up the exercising.

In meditation, there can be no unique restrict as to how lengthy you need to have interaction in the technique. But if you're a amateur, you need to start at a shorter term.

Maybe 5-10 minutes. But as you progress, you could growth the duration. You can use an alarm clock if you want to set a selected time.

8. Meditate regularly.

How frequently want to you do meditation? Well, there is no exceptional technique to this query. But meditating at the least five minutes every day can be beneficial and profitable.

Meditation is the best manner of fun your frame and thoughts. Not to mention its advantages in treating psychological problems which include pressure, despair, and anxiety. Above all, it's miles unfastened. Start meditation nowadays and experience its powerful effect on your well-being.

I choice that this exercise will assist you remove your issues. If you are frightened of a positive event to your lifestyles, just pause for a 2nd and meditate. If you do it proper, you'll gain from it.

thirteen. Have Pets

Having pets in your house can be beneficial in lots of factors. Several studies had determined that domesticating animals can beautify intellectual fitness.

In fact, a meta-evaluation decided six advantages human beings can get from having pets.

1. People who've pets are extra calm and supportive.

2. Pets ought to inform people every time they will be in a volatile state of affairs

three. Pets may additionally want to divert human beings's interest from horrible mind to positivity.

four. People may additionally need to stay active with the useful resource of playing with their pets.

five. Pets have to assist people to stay high-quality.

6. Pets should offer reputation or unconditional excessive great regard.

But what type of animals you want to rear? Most human beings select puppies. But the studies findings located that rearing one-of-a-kind animals which encompass cats have the same advantages.

In illustrating the connection amongst pets and highbrow fitness, the first writer of the have a look at, Dr. Helen Brooks believed that having pets ought to alleviate highbrow fitness troubles. "Our assessment shows that pets provide benefits to human beings with intellectual health conditions," said Brooks.

Interacting with pets can cast off tension and stress. A pet may want to make the proprietor glad and inspired.

The association between pets and highbrow fitness

Aside from blessings said above, pets have an immediate effect on mental fitness.

1. Pets can curtail melancholy

Depression, inside the most effective experience, is an severe loneliness. Depressed human beings need assist in tuning their intellectual reputation again to positivity. One of the extraordinary strategies to enhance mental fitness is rearing pets.

Many people felt like they gain some element giant of their lives at the same time as worrying their pets. They experience tranquillity and find out purpose.

2. Pets can make you more sociable

Walking puppies, for example, will result in conversations. When you are within the park strolling together along with your dogs, you may likely meet wonderful canine owners. Thus, your chance of getting new friends is excessive. And having extra social interactions and relationships can bring about a extra wholesome well-being.

Rearing a home canine does not great make you happy but moreover help protect the animals' welfare.

14. Stay Away From Stressed People

A latest have a have a look at found that being with stressed humans can significantly have an impact in your mind's form. This may be the purpose why family individuals of a depressed person are regularly determined to have the equal symptom as the depressed one.

In addition, the have a study furthermore allows the claim of some experts putting ahead that bad humans are contagious. The researchers determined that the effect of strain changed into not handiest apparent on the emotional however also on the natural detail.

The lead author of the preceding have a take a look at, Dr. Toni-Lee Sterley stated the remarkable prevent. "There has been different literature that indicates strain can be transferred – and our have a examine is truely showing the mind is modified with the useful aid of that transferred stress," defined Sterley.

What takes place to the brain when exposed to confused humans? The researchers discovered that "The neurons that manipulate the mind's response to strain confirmed changes in unstressed companions that were identical to those we measured in the forced mice," said Sterley.

This have a study presents to the developing body of scientific evidence which shows that exposing oneself to depressed human beings can be detrimental. So staying a ways from stressed people can be the incredible thing to do. But how can we understand if a person is stressed-out?

There are commonplace behaviors that a burdened man or woman has a bent to do all of the time. Here are some of the symptoms that a person is burdened-out.

1. Share personal hassle too much

Venting can be beneficial. In truth, it's miles one of the best types of remedy. Talking to a pal can sincerely reduce the burden internal.

However, harassed human beings do it excessively. They cognizance an excessive amount of on their horrible evaluations. And the storytelling may fit on endlessly. Those people have problems in letting skip their terrible past evaluations.

2. Worry too much about the matters they're capable of't control

At a few point in our life, we encounter setbacks. It's a part of being human. Healthy people without a doubt study and drift on.

But forced people can't do this. They typically commonly tend to live on matters they will be capable of't change. As a stop result, they regularly discover themselves in their self-imposed cage.

3. Eat unstable food

Maybe you moreover may additionally observed it – compelled human beings will be predisposed to consume an excessive amount of. This is the motive why no longer all depressed humans are skinny. Some of them are surely fats.

What is worse approximately it is that maximum compelled humans eat horrific materials. They have a tendency to divert their hobby to meals hoping that they neglect their issues or frustrations.

4. Get startled effortlessly

Stressed humans may also effortlessly get beaten. A moderate worrying state of affairs may be a big deal to them.

5. Can't get sufficient sleep

We all revel in it particularly whilst there's masses of factors taking place in our mind – we're able to't sleep.

But harassed human beings can't get sufficient sleep nearly continuously. Their thoughts is whole of exaggerated negative perceptions.

6. Do many stuff concurrently

Most parents make schedules on a daily chores. The cause of scheduling is to preserve topics prepared and maximized our time and resources.

Stressed humans do it in a unique manner. Instead of doing obligations as scheduled, they generally tend to carry out the chores concurrently.

As predicted, they will be exhausted on the surrender of the day. The awful difficulty approximately their dependancy is that they frequently devote mistakes. And self-depreciating terms will pass on.

7. Never ask for assist

Healthy people ask for help whilst they'll be no longer satisfactory what they may be doing. Stressed-out people don't do it. They normally will be inclined to carry out matters on their non-public even though they badly want assist.

8. Focus on the horrible trouble of an revel in

What makes a terrible or specific revel in isn't always the enjoy in keeping with se however how we interpret our experience. A rational character will popularity on the terrific aspect of an occasion in choice to at the horrible.

Stressed people do the opportunity. What they frequently see is the terrible facet not the fine. Because their thoughts is complete of negativities, their terms can also be horrible.

nine. Easily get procrastinated

At some aspect in our lifestyles, we sense procrastination. But if you are a extremely good man or woman, you discover techniques to get brought on.

But careworn-out human beings, due to the fact their thoughts is already full of negativity, they'll effortlessly get discouraged whilst topics did now not skip as deliberate. You first-class see them on the onset of a venture but in the end they will vanish.

10. Always in a rush

Stressed people tend to be hurry all the time. You see them rushing however accomplish now not something. At the quit of the day, they appearance too worn-out however in no manner completed a undertaking. If you spot some of the ones trends of a person, perhaps he/she is burdened-out.

To keep away from being affected, it is proper for you in case you without a doubt live away. Focus on your very personal dreams. Keep regular.

15. Laugh

For centuries, people sought to find out eternal happiness. Everyone desires to be glad. However, in maximum times, becoming glad is a hard issue to do. The cause why maximum people don't discover happiness is that we are trying to find it within the wrong vicinity.

Most people will be predisposed to discover happiness from material subjects. This is a incorrect area to begin. Because happiness can't be placed at the out of doors – it emanates from the inside. If you need to be happier, you don't want to find out your outer international. You as a substitute need to invite your self what certainly makes you happy.

For many human beings, happiness is elusive. But contrary to the common belief, turning into happier is much less complex than you observed. In fact, in modern-day clinical finding, researchers positioned that people who snigger at themselves are happier. In addition, dad and mom which can be humorous had been additionally discovered to be greater sociable.

The key proper here is not the humour itself however the functionality to use humour to snort at oneself. People who're able to laughing their very own imperfections are psychologically greater healthful.

The first author of the check, Jorge Torres Martin defined the prevent give up end result. "… a more tendency to rent self-defeating humour is indicative of immoderate rankings in psychological nicely-being dimensions together with happiness and, to a lesser quantity, sociability," said Martin.

Of path, not all humour can make human beings happier. Some may additionally additionally want to hurt super's feelings. For instance, competitive humour is typically utilized by angry people to specific their anger. Most folks that use aggressive humour are those who have horrible opinions.

The high-quality implication of the take a look at is which you don't need to be remarkable, or have the whole thing to be happier. What you need is laughter. Be appreciative of the subjects round you. Welcome happiness. Open your coronary heart with positivity. If you actually need to be happier for your life, you'll collect it.

sixteen. Develop Self-Compassion

Stress is one of the most perennial highbrow fitness troubles. Most humans's lives are affected by it. If stress isn't managed or monitored, it will negatively have an impact on your regular capability to characteristic on a each day foundation.

In reality, stress has been related to hundreds of mental and bodily issues. It can result in melancholy, coronary coronary heart disorder, immoderate blood strain, or maybe stroke. Untreated strain can break lives. But the extraordinary information is that destroying pressure is only a be counted of preference.

It technique that the brilliant remedy may be placed in you. This claim is supported thru way of a scientific evidence. A agency of researchers located that the best manner to harm pressure is self-compassion. People who preserved love for themselves were decided to be much less stress than their contrary numbers.

In addition, self-compassionate human beings are high-quality, active, and lively. The contributors of the have a look at have been university green individuals. The researchers believed that the transition from excessive school to college is what makes university students pressure.

And they have been proper. Professor Peter Crocker, the co-creator of the take a look at showed the result. "Research suggests the primary-yr college is demanding."

First-12 months college college students will be inclined to address such a number of matters similarly to handling the cutting-edge day surroundings. "Students who are used to getting excessive grades can be shocked to now not do as well in college, enjoy challenged dwelling a ways from home, and are regularly missing important social that that they'd in excessive university," Crocker stated.

But students can constantly deal with stress effects if they understand a manner to do it. The finding shows the first-rate way to spoil stress in college. "Self-compassion seems to be an effective approach or useful resource to cope with the ones kinds of issues," Crocker delivered.

The importance of this have a test isn't simplest constrained to college students. People in all walks of life can benefit from this finding. Stress often takes vicinity even as you fall short of your intention or popular. The exceptional element you can do is avoid being perfect. Accept the truth. Like distinctive humans, you aren't first-class. You make errors.

Don't too tough on yourself. Forgive. Develop self-compassion. That's the quickest manner to damage strain before it destroys you.

17. Smell Your Partner's Shirt

There are many tactics to manipulate pressure. But presently, a new and brilliant locating was located. You is probably amazed, but it's far a systematic truth. A research from the University of British Columbia posted inside the Journal of Personality and Social Psychology located that a scent of a romantic accomplice can lower strain diploma.

The researchers positioned that once uncovered to their companions' heady scent, girls experience greater cushty. In evaluation, whilst uncovered to strangers' heady scent, their stage of stress hormone, cortisol, will growth.

The give up turned into drawn from 96 contrary-intercourse couples participated in the have a have a look at. In the study, male participants have been cautioned to wear a T-blouse for twenty-four hours without using body scented merchandise on the aspect of deodorant. Cigarettes and terrific meals that might have an effect on their perfume have been additionally confined.

The researchers gave the T-shirts of the male contributors to ladies. Then women fragrance the shirt given to them. They were now not informed which blouse is their husband's.

Women additionally underwent a series of strain tests. It concerned a mock challenge interview and highbrow math mission. Then the researchers measured the quantity of cortisol in their saliva. The finding indicates that ladies who smelled their associate's fragrance had a decrease level of strain hormone compared to folks that smelled the stranger's blouse.

What to do at the same time as you're burdened out? Smell your accomplice's blouse. But what makes it paintings? Why exposing to the stranger's fragrance makes humans confused out?

The authors speculate that our early worry of strangers must have caused this hormonal reaction. Children are frightened of a stranger, in particular male strangers. The researchers agree with that the identical fear may additionally additionally have directed the quit result of the take a look at.

However, the take a look at handiest targeted on women. We don't comprehend if the equal finding exists amongst men. Should guys odor their companion's blouse even as burdened out? This query well properly really worth every other medical research.

Nevertheless, the locating has severa implications. Couples may additionally have a brilliant advantage on this. This is probably useful to people who are separated through the individual of their art work.

The on foot surroundings these days may be greater disturbing than ever. Some people need to excursion to one-of-a-kind towns, or perhaps to unique elements of the area to do their task. Leaving or taking a worn blouse or fabric of the only which you love may be a huge help.

18. Keep a gratitude thoughts-set journal

Every day, make a addiction of writing the subjects that make you happy. Enumerate the matters that you feel thankful for. Write them on your mag. "Being thankful to your advantages cancels out lousy thoughts and worries," says Joni Emmerling, a well-being educate.

To relieve stress speedy is much less pricey. It will not price you a dime. All you need is a touch amount of it gradual, location, and effort.

Everyone desires to be happy. But finding the way to final bliss is kind of normally hard. The global is so stressful that retaining up is even extra difficult.

However, inside the beyond several years, technological information keeps unfolding the elements of happiness. One of the vital members to happiness is gratitude. Perhaps you recognize that gratitude permits us enjoy better, sleep higher, lowers our stress diploma, and makes us extra powerful.

Robert A. Emmons, professor of psychology at UC Davis said that:

"Clinical trials suggest that the exercise of gratitude might also have dramatic and lasting effects in someone's life."

But what are you able to do to enjoy its advantages? In his check posted inside the Journal of Personality and Social Psychology, Emmons located that maintaining a gratitude mag makes humans happier.

After a month of each day journaling, people expanded their subjective happiness through 10 percentage. This happiness stage generally expert by using individuals who were given promoted to their manner.

The end modified into drawn from corporations of people. One enterprise business enterprise changed into counseled to install writing down their every day sports. While the opportunity enterprise modified into told to document some issue that makes them satisfied every day.

The findings propose that individuals inside the gratitude organization had a better stage of delight with their lives than the manage business enterprise. They are more powerful and had a better interpersonal dating with others.

The researchers concluded that "It appears that participation within the gratitude situation triggered big and steady improvements in human beings's tests of the worldwide nicely-being."

Taken the findings into attention, to be happy you don't want perks. All you want is a pen, a pocket e book, and a piece pinch of time.

Write as a minimum 3 to five property you are grateful for each day and the day in advance than. Don't worry approximately the "now not so pinnacle" revel in. Just focus at the positives.

You don't should consider it. Just write the number one effective detail that comes on your mind. The simpler and shorter your sentences, the better. Make it a addiction. Along the way, you may word that the call of the sport to happiness is without a doubt on a paper.

19. Art Therapy

If you may't discover motivation or enjoy stupid and sad, why not strive art work? Art treatment is an expressive therapy that consists of revolutionary undertakings to beautify one's emotion.

The British Association of Art Therapists defined art remedy as "A shape of psychotherapy that makes use of artwork media as its number one mode of conversation. It is practiced via certified registered Art Therapists who paintings with youngsters, greater younger people, adults and the elderly."

During this device, a person makes use of his/her creativity to create some thing resourceful. The top notch issue is you don't need to be an artist to gain benefits from this healing method.

The purpose, therefore, is to in short loosen the stressed thoughts, not looking to be quality. Art therapy is effective in enhancing the temper. A current have a have a look at, for instance, discovered that coloring in books stepped forward humans's emotion.

Dr. Girija Kaimal, the take a look at's leader concluded that "Coloring may allow for some cut price in distress or negativity, however considering the fact that it's miles a based totally project, it might not allow for in addition revolutionary expression, discovery, and exploration which we assume is related to the immoderate excellent temper upgrades we noticed within the open studio situation."

Art treatment does not always involve sketching or drawing. It may be of numerous office paintings. Music is considered one of them. It can be playing musical devices and/or making a song songs. Art remedy does no longer only enhance mood however moreover useful to our health. In truth, a few studies decided that this restoration technique really helped most cancers sufferers.

Having a most cancers is a very stressful enjoy. The emotional war regularly consequences in melancholy. So art work and dance can be beneficial to alleviate pressure, anger, and unhappiness. Although artwork treatment frequently includes expert steerage, it does no longer suggest that you may't be expressive for your personal.

All you need to do is revisit your passion. Believe it or not, there's a creative person indoors you.

20. Change the environment

Light is an crucial element of lifestyles. All residing organisms depend upon this astounding artwork of nature. From plants to animals of all type, mild permits the whole thing to thrive. On humans, lighting fixtures have a extremely good impact now not exceptional at the bodily detail however additionally on feelings.

A contemporary take a look at located an exciting finding. A wonderful colour of lighting modifications emotion. The check of Jesus Minguillon and his colleagues observed that blue light reduces pressure degree 3 times quicker than other everyday white light.

The give up of the have a take a look at have grow to be drawn from 12 people participated in the have a take a look at. The participants have been intentionally forced and divided into same businesses. In the second degree of the test, the people have then handed via relaxation consultation in the chromotherapy room.

One institution was exposed to white moderate, at the same time because the alternative organization have come to be uncovered to blue slight. At the quit of the test, the researchers concluded that those members who've been assigned to the blue mild have been greater snug than the alternative organization.

The authors of the test defined:

"… blue lighting accelerates the relaxation approach after stress in contrast with conventional while lighting.

The relaxation time reduced with the useful aid of approximately three-fold (1.1 vs. Three.Five minutes).

We additionally placed a convergence time (three.5-five mins) and then the benefit of blur lights disappeared."

However, the have a look at become now not the primary medical studies held to recognize the effect of lights on human emotion.

In reality, the authors said comparable studies:

"A take a look at about the have an impact on of color of partitions in reading environments proved that dwindled colors delivered on more rest than super shades, and the coronary heart rate decreased with brief-wavelength shades (e.G., violet, blue and green) in evaluation longer-wavelength (e.G., yellow and crimson).

In addition, some authors have efficaciously dealt with people with behaviour issues with the useful resource of way of influencing their emotional states (e.G., causing highbrow calm) by means of using color lighting.

For instance, red slight became successfully implemented to reduce aggressiveness of delinquents in jail.

Furthermore, every different shade-lighting-based method with blue moderate were used for disruptive behaviour issues…"

The locating can be useful now not only for experts but furthermore to each person. A smooth blue lighting in our house can also moreover need to reduce pressure level.

21. Visit Mother Nature

The contemporary-day international is worrying and chaotic making happiness elusive. That's why maximum human beings discover it difficult to be satisfied. The proper information is that you can be satisfied no matter your present day fact. Happiness isn't always a commodity. It is some problem without problems available.

But most human beings don't recognise it. Becoming happier every day will not value you a dime. In truth, a cutting-edge study found that spending a second appreciating matters round you is enough to make you feel precise.

A check led my Holli-Anne Passmore placed that taking a smash is useful to shift your temper. In addition, bringing your self to mother-nature should make you even happier. There were 395 humans participated in the look at. The individuals have been divided into 3 groups.

One agency modified into assigned to take a look at guy-made systems on the identical time because the alternative agency modified into assigned to have a take a look at nature. The emotion of every institution become in comparison to the manipulate organization who did neither. The finding suggests that searching at natural devices collectively with plants and timber decorate properly-being.

Passmore concluded:

"The distinction in individuals' well-being — their happiness, experience of elevation, and their degree of connectedness to different people, not truly nature — grow to be significantly better than individuals inside the institution noticing how human-constructed items made them sense and the control organisation."

This is not the first examine to indicate the huge effect of mother-nature in human emotion. Some studies additionally determined traveling parks can make someone happier. The first rate issue is that you don't want to live for prolonged hours within the park to enjoy particular. You quality want a couple of minutes.

Holli-Anne Passmore added:

"This wasn't about spending hours outdoor or going for lengthy walks within the wilderness. This is ready the tree at a bus prevent in the center of a city and the great effect that one tree could have on humans."

Noticing natural surrounding will no longer only help you experience happier however additionally boosts your prosocial behavior - that is feeling glad assisting others. Next time you experience stressed thru your artwork or courting, try and detach yourself out of your current-day truth. Breathe some glowing air. Visit the park close to you and enjoy the natural splendor of your surroundings.

In so doing, you may be in a position to triumph over tranquillity and happier day! Previously, a have a have a look at in Australia had decided that living in nearby sea shore allows reduce stress and despair incidents. It modified into one of the quantities of proof that factors out the coolest effect of mom-nature in human fitness. Another have a examine solidifies the previous claim. The employer of researchers led with the aid of Ms. Simone Kühn discovered that those who stay nearby forests have greater wholesome mind form specially the amygdala.

The amygdala is a thoughts shape this is liable for processing emotional responses collectively with fear and pressure. The researchers endorse that dwelling close to or among wooden can help lessen strain. The quit have become drawn from the statistics retrieved from the senior people aged sixty one to eighty .

Ms. Simone Kühn, the number one creator concluded:

"Research on mind plasticity enables the idea that the environment can form mind form and function.

That is why we're interested by the environmental conditions that can have excessive splendid effects at the thoughts development.

Studies of people within the geographical area have already tested that dwelling close to nature is right for their intellectual fitness and properly-being.

We, therefore, determined to take a look at city dwellers."

The proof turns into more potent – residing close by mother-nature is proper for the health. It can be that the tranquillity of nature allows the thoughts to lighten up. The relaxed state of thoughts has a incredible effect on the whole human biology.

The co-author of the have a study, Professor Ulman Lindenberger stated:

"Our take a look at investigates the connection amongst city making plans features and thoughts fitness for the number one time.

By 2015, nearly 70 percent of the area populace is anticipated to be dwelling in towns.

These results have to, therefore, be very critical for metropolis making plans.

In the close to destiny, but, the located association many of the thoughts and closeness to forests could want to be confirmed in in addition studies and different towns."

Another implication of the finding is that human beings don't need to spend coins to lighten up. A smooth go to to a public park or wooded region is enough to have a pressure unfastened thoughts and healthful frame.

Chapter 5: 8 Effective Anger Management Techniques

Anger is part of human emotion. It is healthy. We can be indignant if there may be a reason to perform that. However, sometimes it's far hard to govern. The out of manipulate anger can bring about a complicated tendency. Fortunately, regular with a systematic psychologist Isabel Clarke, "You can control your anger, and you've got a responsibility to perform that."

Anger is one of the maximum powerful human feelings. So controlling it could be hard. Here are the useful suggestions you could do while you are angry.

Anger manipulate strategies

Isabel Clarke has a caution: "Everyone has a reaction to anger. Be aware of what your frame is telling you, and take steps to calm your self down."

This technique that anger is predictable. You understand what makes you indignant and at the equal time as you probably get angry. And because you could assume your conduct, it may be smooth to format an motion plan. Here's what you may do.

1. Be aware about your anger symptoms and signs and symptoms

You comprehend the signs and symptoms that you are irritated. Your respiratory and heartbeat end up quicker. Your jaw and fists are clenching. This may imply which you are about to supply a devastating movement. Isabel Clarke shows that: "If you word those signs and symptoms, get out of the state of affairs if you've were given a information of dropping manipulate."

Avoidance is now and again the most effective way. Don't wait till you can not manage your very very own emotion. Take motion as quick as possible.

2. Count 1 to ten

This might also sound funny, but it could be useful. Counting to ten allows you remove your motion. And extra importantly, helps you to evaluate the possible very last results of your behavior more as it have to be and constructively.

three. Slow down your breathing

One of the best anger control techniques is slowing your respiration down. Yes, if you may manipulate your breathing, you could control your mood. Isabel introduced, "You automatically breathe in greater than out whilst you are feeling irritated, and the trick is to respire out extra than in. This will calm you down efficaciously and assist you receive as genuine with you studied extra virtually."

4. Exercise

Another way to effectively deal your anger is to engage in bodily sports activities sports consisting of exercising. Walking, strolling, swimming, and outside sports activities sports can be effective to reduce your mood. "Exercise as a part of your every day existence is a outstanding manner to do away with inflammation and anger," says Isabel Clarke.

five. Take care of your self

Anger is every now and then a combination of stress and self-indifference. You are busy taking care the desires of others whilst forgetting your private desires. So looking after your self could make you calm. Why now not take a vacation and loosen up. Get sufficient sleep and stay from pills, caffeine, and alcohol. These chemical compounds are people to pressure. In truth, Isabel Clarke says that "They lower inhibitions and, clearly, we need inhibitions to forestall us acting unacceptably even as we're irritated."

6. Make something thrilling

Your hobbies can be a large help to calm your anger. One of the powerful anger manipulate techniques may be writing, dancing, portray, creating a tune and song writing. These sports lessen anger and physical anxiety.

7. Express your feeling

Sharing your emotions with others may be beneficial to reduce your emotional burden. And extra importantly, you may get first-rate people involved in formulating effective treatments.

8. Free yourself from any anger inflicting mind

Sometimes, anger emanates out of your thoughts. If you hold on considering how unwanted a state of affairs is, you cannot put off it. That's why Isabel Clarke shows that "Try to allow move of any unhelpful strategies of thinking. Thoughts which includes 'It's no longer truthful,' or 'People like that have to no longer be on the roads,' ought to make anger worse."

To free yourself from any negative mind, try and avoid the following phrases:

- "You in no way be aware of me."

- "I want to be on time."

- "The global isn't always fair."

- "You have to continuously do what I want."

Chapter 6: 20 Magical Steps to Happiness

With all the worrying situations we face each day, each in university or at work, it is able to be tough to experience happiness. The global is an increasing number of annoying and complex. Our every day recurring occasionally becomes toxic to our mental and physical fitness.

But the good data is that no matter how horrible your experience may be, there's constantly a room for happiness. You may be satisfied if you need to. Stress is simplest a made from your evaluation. That is in case you think that an occasion is annoying, it is truly annoying.

Your mind performs a great function in the manner you understand your international. If you fill it bad imaginings, you'll not be able to recognize the beauty round you. So one manner of accomplishing eternal happiness is knowing that strain is a end result of a faulty cognitive evaluation.

Once you change the manner you understand your revel in, you'll be capable of accumulate healthful questioning sample. Happiness also can have fantastic meanings to crucial people. Our kind of reviews and emotions lead us to provide you with a selected statistics of happiness. For centuries, philosophers, theologians, and psychologists sought to define this emotional country. Thus, this collect earns particular meanings.

However, some interpretations are greater honest than the alternative. The commonplace interpretation is that happiness is a mental kingdom of well-being that comprises outstanding feelings. People who have a exquisite assessment in their modern-day lifestyles's fact have a tendency to be happy.

But the actual question isn't always how we outline happiness; it's far how we come to be glad. How people in our generation feel nicely approximately themselves? In the arena of hate, discrimination, and judgment, happiness becomes elusive. It will become a precious commodity that maximum humans can't find out the coins for.

Fortunately, happiness is unfastened. This is the reality. We honestly select to miss approximately this truth. And we join the idea that lifestyles is tough and whole of struggles. While in fact, it is not. Here are the easy steps in becoming satisfied to your existence.

1. Wish extraordinary matters for others

Are you affected thru a effective bodily contamination? Do you be with the aid of financial debt? Or, do you have got problems together with your modern courting? Maybe you're questioning that all you enjoy at gift is horrible. That is why you envy extraordinary people. But you interpret it wrong. In fact, you are at the right time to need the exceptional for them. Because looking the splendid for others can provide you with happiness. The feeling of delight maximum of the time comes from your external global. It is an act of being associated and worried with others. If you sense satisfied about the achievements of others, unconsciously you feel internal satisfaction. That's the manner to actual happiness.

2. Pretend which you already accumulate the belongings you want to accumulate

What it's miles which you really need to gain? Is it a pleasing automobile, a powerful relationship, a university degree, or a monetary fulfillment? Most humans caught within the idea that turning into successful is difficult. They regularly forget about about that they have got what it takes to be glad and a success. If you want to gain fulfillment to your existence, you need to pretend as a successful individual already. It may also additionally sound stupid, but it's far true. Hold your goal for your mind very actually. What I imply by using this is that during case you need a steeply-priced vehicle, make a addiction of continuously considering that automobile. Imagine which you are the use of it. This method lets in you creates recognition of your proper capability. Most humans overlook about that they've the simplest tool - their thoughts. Whatever the thoughts conceives, it will become a fact.

3. Appreciate the splendor of everything

Most of the time we attention on horrible activities or topics in our existence. As a give up stop result, we infrequently be aware the top notch subjects around us. We overlook approximately that during each poor occasion, there is a nice component of it. So to gain happiness, try and recognition on immoderate brilliant matters. Find a few trouble that makes you experience satisfaction. Is it a bit of song? A portray? A poem or novel? Just pass spherical and apprehend matters that make you happy.

four. Build well relationship with others

There are many things which can make someone happy. Money is one in each of them. But financial achievement isn't always the handiest predictor of happiness. Some research of happiness located that right dating is what makes us glad. Of course, a relationship entails a top reference to different humans. It can be an intimate courting or a dating along aspect your dad and mom and massive others. In reality, the properly-being of an entire united states of america is quite relying on social ties now not in a right economic machine.

five. Maintain super thoughts

Whatever you do, hold a awesome strength that flows for your body. What I mean with the resource of the use of that is that you need to have in thoughts of your thoughts. Avoid terrible wondering. It poisons your properly-being. Because when you have doubts in your very personal functionality, then you will prevent your very motive. Negative people do now not obtain their desires. Why? Because they assume they cannot. The 2nd you suspect you can't you can not achieve your goal. Remember that some thing you positioned becomes your reality.

6. Find peace in you

Happiness emanates from having determined your self in straightforward judgment. Let pass of these lousy evaluations. Whatever came about the previous day does now not truely have an impact on your present. Learn to forgo topics which can be out of your manipulate. And remain hopeful. Start building your amazing destiny. If you keep for your bad imaginings, you could find out your self in sadness. Thus, attempt to find peace no matter your cutting-edge-day truth.

7. Maximize your ability

Most humans forget approximately who they clearly are. They expect that they can't achieve a few detail. But the reality is they will be greater capable than they expect. The simplest detail that holds them back from attaining achievement is their self-proclaimed weak spot - their bad thoughts. In addition, they don't comprehend that they've a incredible amount of ability. If you really need to stay a happy life, you have got got to make use of your capability. Make dreams in recent times and paintings on them.

8. Decide to be a glad person

The closing manner to end up glad is to determine to accumulate happiness. If you're a person who desperately wants to be satisfied and but you fill yourself with hatred and envy, you couldn't advantage happiness. In order to enjoy pleasure, you need to set yourself loose from terrible emotions. And it takes courage to do it. It is extra than wearing a grin each day, it is dwelling in a pleasant emotional nation.

nine. Never blame

Whenever you fail on a few issue or completed a few errors in your desire, do no longer blame all people or something. Just be given failure and studies from it. Find methods to solve your trouble constructively. Focus at the subjects that you could do now not on what you cannot. Blaming is a waste of time and power. Be clever sufficient.

10. Give what is essential

Most people have goals. But the problem is that the artwork they offer to acquire the ones desires is not same to what is needed. Higher goals want extra and more difficult paintings. If there may be a huge discrepancy amongst your purpose and your try, you may not be successful. It is essential which you supply the important attempt.

11. Spend time in silence

The top notch vicinity to find happiness is in silence. Find some time to unplug your self from the noisy international. Make reflections of your self. Picture on your thoughts all the exceptional things that happened to your life so far. What are the ones? And what are the ones which you need to accumulate in the future? Silence permits you connect to the invisible forces spherical you. Spend time to conquer happiness.

12. Be privy to your physical fitness

You cannot separate highbrow health from bodily health. A disturbed mind should negatively have an effect on the frame. And the ill frame also can have an impact at the thoughts. In this tenet, you can not attain right happiness when you have bodily troubles. Many research located that adults who be afflicted through physical ailments have horrific intellectual health. The maximum affected intellectual feature is subjected properly-being.

The satisfactory problem to do is asking after your frame. Avoid terrible meals which encompass speedy elements, gentle beverages, and many others. Exercise every day and boom an early slumbering agenda.

Staying overdue at night time time time will negatively have an impact for your physical and highbrow fitness.

thirteen. Avoid overthinking

To end up a happy individual, you need to unfastened your mind from overthinking. Overthinking takes place on the equal time as you fear an excessive amount of about a future event. You are making an exaggerated evaluation of a few issue that is uncertain. It will not do any pinnacle.

In order to conquer happiness, you need to make a logical evaluation. Do no longer stress your self to take manipulate of something that you don't have any functionality to advantage this. Picture your future with need and pleasure. Let glide of your problems and allow your tomorrow spread itself. By accepting your problem, you'll be able to unfastened your mind from overthinking.

14. Make a list of your little achievements

Either you trust it or not, you're conducting adorable topics every day. But maximum humans don't understand it. All they see is frustrations and defeat. If you want to become satisfied, you want to apprehend every little fulfillment or improvement you're making on a each day basis.

You can do it with the useful resource of making a list. Make a addiction of writing down your little achievements. It will not best make you glad but moreover remind you methods masses you've already completed. Just keep in thoughts that the only way to get in your reason is by means of the usage of way of doing small acts each day. And those small quantities of movements will sum up into a big triumph.

15. Smile

It is awesome to understand that generation discovered out that a simple smile is useful. When you smile the quantity of serotonin on your mind will boom. Serotonin is a neurotransmitter or a chemical in the mind that enhances mood. Every day, discover a cause to do it. Watch your preferred comedy movie or find a person who makes you laugh. This clean act is sufficient to grow to be a satisfied man or woman.

16. Be grateful

For years, ordinary humans and scientists are locating the very last manner toward accomplishing happiness. Many of the research recommend that turning into happy is truely free. In reality, a studies finding placed that happiness comes from being thankful in your little achievements.

People who make a listing of factors they may be thankful for are happier than parents that don't. The well problem is that every day there are plenty of proper matters show up to you. The handiest trouble is that you chose now not to look them. What you generally generally tend to appearance are the horrible sports. If you really need to emerge as a happy character, try to recognize little correct topics on your lifestyles.

17. Surround yourself with happy people

Stress is contagious. If you need to be satisfied, avoid bad people. They can't help you. Instead, discover tremendous people who can excite your day. They don't handiest make you satisfied, however moreover encourage you to get going.

18. Play together collectively with your pets

Your domestic dog can enhance your happiness. Many research discovered that individuals who rear pets are happier than those who do now not have pets. Animal enthusiasts have a propensity to have better subjective happiness.

19. Don't watch the news

If you're looking the statistics on TV and one in every of a type media, possibilities are you furthermore mght observed that your probabilities of viewing first-rate facts are lesser than viewing terrible data. In different phrases, you seldom see actual statistics inside the media. The terrible issue is that bad statistics will act as a plague. It will cloud your mind till your perception of the world may additionally moreover grow to be terrible.

If you actually need to grow to be a satisfied character, flip off your TV and don't take note of the terrible facts. Instead, respect all the great things that happened to you within the whole day. This will make you comfortable and satisfied.

20. Forgive and overlook

We are all site visitors. And alongside the manner, we meet people who make us satisfied and/or irritated. In fact, in worse times, people would likely belittle us or demean us. But a few element happens, do not live on anger and vengeance. The first-rate problem to do is to forgive and overlook. Forget all of the folks that harm you. Focus in your goals. Be indifferent to what others might be pronouncing about you. Through this, you'll emerge as happier.

Chapter 7: 6 Secrets to Become Happier

Happiness is one of the most debated ideas in social technological knowledge. From philosophy to psychology, happiness has given severa interpretations. However, irrespective of its complexity, everyone, in some unspecified time inside the future has skilled happiness. It is a totally satisfied feeling that makes us experience great. As a end quit result, we need to cling to that feeling.

But the arena turns into increasingly more complicated. The way we live has changed. Happiness has become elusive. Life appears difficult, as what maximum humans accept as true with. Happiness has grow to be a commodity that only a few could have enough cash.

But, the fact is exactly the opportunity. Happiness isn't always some thing to pursue. Rather, it's far some detail to select. In truth, some happiness researchers accept as true with that happiness is an issue of preference. And we will do that by way of approach of choosing the proper mind - the superb ones. And via retaining off the awful imaginations.

Thus, it isn't always a query of what makes us glad but how willing we are to be happy. The most crucial attention proper right right here is that everyone can gain a satisfied lifestyles. If, and handiest if s/he chooses to be glad.

At this time, I will talk a number of the secrets and strategies and techniques of happiness. If you recognize and take a look at those gadgets in your lifestyles, you could come to be a happier character.

1. Happy life is a sum of happiness

That's proper. In order to be happy, you should choose to be satisfied with none fear. Of path, lifestyles is continuously difficult. You continuously will be inclined to fulfill your each day desires. And that requires lots of attempt. If succeeded, you'll revel in true. If no longer, you may feel bitter and fear extra. But if you check it in a high-quality manner, you can see that there is enough motive to enjoy right.

The exceptional thing you can do while matters are going incorrect is to evaluate whether or not or now not or no longer you have got got were given a few shape of control over those things. Assessment permits you hundreds in shaping your emotion. Because in case you do now not have manipulate over the topics that grew to turn out to be incorrect, then you haven't any motive to be sad.

It is everyday to revel in lousy at the same time as a state of affairs is horrific, however you want to rescue yourself out of that emotion. You want to teach your thoughts in the method of turning into happy.

Happiness isn't always all about terrific existence's times, however a top notch outlook on the topics that take area to you. Sadness cannot remedy chaos. You cannot repair what is damaged by means of manner of retaining yourself imprisoned in negative emotions. You are actually placing heavy loads to your shoulder. So find out motives to be glad. 2. Happy lifestyles is a grateful lifestyles

Hatred reduces your tendency to emerge as satisfied. Happiness starts offevolved offevolved on the identical time as you exercise gratitude. Be thankful for the whole thing that happened to you. For everything you have got - a pleasing circle of relatives, buddies and first rate others. In this manner, you neglect negativity and foster happiness in you.

three. Happy life is prepared forgiveness

Living in frustration and hatred will confine you to awful emotion - disappointment. And awful emotion can significantly impact your intellectual health. That's why folks that preserve grudges and anger are much more likely to build up fitness problems. It is everyday to experience unhappy and angry, however you have to unfastened yourself from those feelings as rapid as you may. And begin giving forgiveness for folks who did wrong unto you. This may additionally sound less tough but it is not. It requires an sincere willpower.

In order to region forgiveness into action, you want to place yourself inside the footwear of the perpetrators. Try to apprehend why they did it to you. This method will can help you resolve your one-sided assessment. And from hatred, attempt to be altruistic. Be inclined to forgo and forget about about things for the blessings of others. And you'll end up happier than ever!

four. Happiness is a thoughts complete of pleasure

Happiness is a crafted from high-quality thinking. If you've got happy evaluation about your lifestyles, you may be satisfied. Therefore, you can not advantage happiness with the resource of the utilization of getting horrible mind.

If you phrase that you're going to be horrific, shift your questioning. Challenge that perception via using asking the reason inside the lower back of. Is it critical to experience sad or aggravated? This will will will let you break out from forming terrible thoughts.

Why is it crucial to test out bad mind? Well, the human thoughts acts like a magnet. It draws the like. So awesome thoughts attract exceptional situation. If you're satisfied, you lure satisfied humans. But if you are indignant, you will appeal to awful angry humans. This is what they called The Law of Attraction. The regulation of attraction moreover suggests that being happy helps you reap your dreams in lifestyles.

five. Happy lifestyles does no longer rely on cash

At some aspect, coins ought to make you happy. But actually, money isn't the fine hassle of happiness. It is the connection that topics the maximum. It may be a dating together together with your parents, buddies, siblings, co-personnel, and lots of others. Not coins. This is the reason why most people in 0.33 global international locations although revel in happiness while no longer having more money. To grow to be happy, you simply need to fee the relationship which you have with others. Be thankful and cherish the moments together with your circle of relatives.

6. Happy life is all approximately having appropriate social connection

Humans are social animals. You can not stay on my own. You are a part of the widely widespread net. And the excellent element about this is that being related with others make you satisfied. Your possibility to find out buddies is extremely good. The more buddies you have, the happier you could emerge as.

So assemble a excellent courting with others. Cherish the instances on your life along side your circle of relatives. To me, happiness is the final because of this of life. People who live in a lifestyles entire of hatred and frustrations are the oldsters that don't get the real that means in their existence.

In life, it isn't always how masses you have got were given, it is the way you fee what you've got. This is the way to gain happiness.

Chapter 8: CAUSES OF STRESS

Stress has innumerable and varied reasons; the reasons are almost too many to be listed. However, the most effective reasons are individuals who stem from our ideals and thoughts. There are so many stereotyped beliefs that reason strain than you'll accept as true with. In this economic catastrophe, I could be exploring these numerous resources of strain in case you need to assisting the reader take due care or respect the manner to a amazing recovery.

Conformity, Comparison and Competition

Societal stereotypes abound. Wherever we turn, there is usually an expectation of perfection, in seems, wealth, achievement, possessions and plenty of others. To which we're predicted to comply. These stereotypes are on the TVs, your Facebook Timeline and Instagram newsfeeds, on posters in the department stores, on billboards inside the cities. And we heed these calls genuinely, taking the bait. We then trouble ourselves with turning into exactly like what we're continuously tested because the signal of perfection. You need to start to fear masses approximately your appears, think your brains out about your shape, and spend all of the money you've got on cosmetics.

From mere societal stereotypes comes the need to test ourselves with the so-known as archetypes after which a blind competition even among ourselves toward achieving our new-newsfeeds determined goal of conformity to societal stereotypes. Thus, you could engage in unwise spending or mission your physical abilties to the ultimate possible limit. In short, your purpose of conforming to requirements can then make you harassed out.

Negative Changes to Our Lives

Another supply of strain in our lives are fast or foremost changes in our lifestyle. These modifications are commonly now not up to us to govern. It might be a break up. It is probably that you actually misplaced your assignment, elevated financial responsibilities, a demise inside the own family and so forth. The list is endless. In such instances as above, it isn't always uncommon to discover ourselves careworn out.

Space, Time and Mind Cluttering

This may be cut up into vicinity muddle, time clutter and then mind muddle. Space clutter takes place on the same time as we top off our immediately location, domestic or workplace, with mindless and vain stuff. An empty area in the residence isn't a signal of lack however such empty regions which might be supposed to contribute to our accurate fitness are clearly full of materials, way to our new consumer manner of life.

Time clutter refers to taking up extra engagements than you can pretty address. This is typically so because of the reality we constantly find out it tough to say "No" to fine human beings or because of the truth we equate taking over greater responsibilities with productiveness. The impact of that is that we become crushed through how plenty we've taken on, thereby getting ourselves greater worked up than is critical.

Mind cluttering refers to that kingdom in which you have piled up such quite a few pressing topics into the finite region that is your mind. It occurs at the same time as you use up everything of your intellectual skills and fill it up with useless sources of strain. Worry and anxiety are dominant emotions at the same time as the thoughts is cluttered up.

The listing of motives of strain is form of inexhaustible however the ones highlighted above are the maximum famous, and can also capture simply all particular feasible reasons of stress.

Chapter 9: HOW STRESS AFFECTS YOU

What occurs even as we give up the reins of our lives to pressure? What takes region when we refuse, whether or not or not with the resource of mistake or format, to do something effective about stress? Will our lives be the better off? No, in no way! If we go away stress to take over our lives, a few thing which may be pretty gradual as rain clouds stealthily cover up the radiance of the solar, the impact on our lives isn't always so extraordinary in any respect.

The outcomes of not solving pressure variety from power drain, via Unproductivity to violence. You ought to do some thing to deal with an excessive amount of stress. But earlier than then, it is better to first recognize how pressure negatively impacts our lives and this is the point of interest of this bankruptcy.

Energy Drain

Energy, the ability or strength to do paintings or make the effort, or the liveliness and forcefulness in us, our power is a very vital human commodity. Energy is crucial to our life; it is the lifestyles in us. It is what lets in us to transport from one area to a few other. It offers us the power of speech, supporting us float every muscle inside the neck vital to communicate our thoughts to others, no matter the reality that with out our conscious involvement.

Going to the mall may were not possible with energy. All the time we spend with our family, play fetch with Jack, the canine or building a sand fort on the beach, all of those are due to the lifestyles pressure, the electricity that cusses all over our frame. But whilst stress gadgets in, one of the subjects that occurs to us is that we lose our strength. Yes, stress is an energy drain. We are like a tub tub and power is just like the water with which it is stuffed. However, at the same time as stress becomes our fact, the plug which holds the water inside the bath begins to be lifted frequently, permitting drops of water out on the start, till it's far simply lifted from the drain and the water goes out faster than it got here to be within the bath. Stress, luxurious reader, is an power drain.

Once we permit strain to linger in our lives, the primary factor we face is an electricity drain. We begin to lose the strength to do, the capability to make attempt. Activities approximately which we were pleased a short even as earlier than then turn out to be arduous ones, requiring loads try to finish. But what has modified? The activities? No! It is us that have modified. After experiencing electricity drain due to drain, the strength left in us is truly too little simply so sports activities that would mainly require little electricity to finish now seem to require a lot.

Time Drain

This is the second effect of stress on our lives, and it follows logically from experiencing electricity drain. Time drain, to be positioned truely, refers to dropping time. But if time is not like chips, if time is not material, how are we able to lose it? While I intend not to go into the philosophy of time proper here, it suffices to mention that by means of the usage of time drain, I advise you spend time that you in the vital might have used to complete one component or the alternative, including completing the extremely-cutting-edge research to enhance a proposal at paintings, doing now not whatever particularly. Or, you discover yourself spending big swathes of time doing subjects with too little terrific end result.

Time is the first-class useful aid we've got as people. It is a resource which can never be regained as quickly as out of place. Last week is lengthy beyond and is by no means coming yet again. And reality be knowledgeable, it's miles a fallacy to assume all and sundry have it in identical degree. While all and sundry have twenty-4 hours within the day, some of us have the ones hours scheduled for others, whether or not or no longer for a pay or with out cost. And a few others, they pay others to get their private hours loose. Yet, in whichever of the two stated education we fall, one component is excessive excellent: all people have a finite amount of time to ourselves.

It is that amount of time that strain drains, dropping it away earlier than our very eyes. Why? Because you have were given had been given given the a ways flung control of your lifestyles to strain. And for so long as pressure holds sway, reigning first-rate in our lives, our freedom will live greater illusory than a mirage.

Unproductivity

Unproductivity is the shortage of capability to be inexperienced. It makes all logical sense that that is what follows electricity and time drain. Stress is one way to make certain we are unproductive. Productivity relies upon on topics: having the power, the existence in us to exert efforts, intellectual or physical; and , having the desired time inner which to utilise the said energy. But, as I actually have said above, expensive reader, one cannot mistake the reality of productiveness while one lets in stress to control one's existence.

With stress removing the wished power to exert efforts and the time inner which to exert the stated efforts, what is inevitable is that we discover it difficult, at the start, to offer out our fantastic. What is our nice continues escaping us frequently till what we deliver is in truth as correct as not anything.

At this degree, we have come to be honestly unproductive, way to pressure!

Depression

After the fact of unproductivity hits us like lightening, like a thunderbolt, what afflicts us subsequent is a revel in of displeasure with ourselves, a experience of disappointment and maximum problematically, a sense of hopelessness. Yes, I am talking about despair. In fact, you may hold from the moderate feeling of sadness and hopelessness proper into a rustic to be able to require medical interest. But, proper here, on this ebook, as I actually have said in advance on, I offer an answer in advance than you pass the Rubicon.

Do not permit pressure drag you all of the way all the manner down to the bottomless pit of despair. Why? From pressure, you pass from a existence with a whole lot meaning to little that means after which ultimately no meaning. You lose now not only yourself however furthermore sight of humanity. Stress, if left unchecked, can bring about the dominion in which the vilest in man is made take vicinity.

Violence

What takes area even as we permit strain to take the reins of our lives to such quantity as purpose us to lose sight of no longer handiest ourselves however additionally of what makes us human? He that unearths no that means in life will discover no such which means for others. He grade by grade loses what makes him humane until he gives in without problems to his heat passion, now not restraining himself in violence toward his fellow man. I am sorry if that sounds a bit poetic. I in reality couldn't keep in mind a better way to provide an cause of how strain can drag us fast into the jewelry of violence.

The violence we speak approximately right right right here is not best prolonged inside the route of others however moreover in the direction of ourselves as undergo the stress. If this receives worse, there need to be a skinny fabric between us and our non-public lives. Hence, some thing ought to be completed approximately stress. But what are we able to stand to gain fixing pressure? The answer to this can be the point of interest of the following economic disaster on this ebook.

Are you playing this ebook to this point? Please go away a examine on amazon if you are.

Click right here to leave a examine for this ebook on Amazon!

Chapter 10: WHY FIX STRESS

Why repair stress? There are matters to consider even as answering this query. In the previous financial ruin, we considered one of those i.E. The terrible results of pressure in our lives. In the preceding financial disaster, we have been made to recognize that if we refuse to restore pressure, if we refuse to do some thing high-quality about it, if we sit down again and allow it take manipulate of our lives, we can now not be the better off. Rather, we can lose frequently the essence of existence, till we had been dragged to the bottom of the low pits of dejectedness and hopelessness, at which degree we become so crushed.

But what are we able to stand to benefit at the same time as we recovery stress? What are the benefits of fixing pressure, putting off it proper at the same time as it comes into our lives or while we discover it? What are we able to stand to gain while we deliver stress packing, refusing itstenancy or lordship in our lives? A amazing deal, of route! This stages from getting greater strength via extra cash to actualising one's golden dream. What are a number of the greater precise blessings you stand to gain?

More Energy

Recall that one of the first subjects strain does to us is to sap us of electricity, to empty the existence out oldsters and what we do. Upon solving pressure, then, one of the blessings can be to regain or to prevent that strength from draining. How does this occur? What in truth saps our strength is the litter in our mind. We have already identified the reasons of stress as thoughts, area and time cluttering. If you could dispose of stress, automatically, you'll have more time, area, and peace of thoughts. This will prevent the worn-out, exhausted united states that usually comes with pressure.

More Time

While we're troubled via the evil palms of pressure, we are vulnerable to a revel in of languor which helps us waste away our time doing not anything. We lose time faster than a basket loses water being poured into it. What this shows is that we permit valuable time we ought to have used for a few detail inexperienced and profitable waste away, after spending the time doing no longer whatever because of inclined factor, because of being uninterested in lifestyles and strength to provide lifestyles into one-of-a-kind topics via our efforts. But as soon as we healing strain, what we enjoy is strong utilisation of time. But it does not truly prevent there. The benefit goes forward to gaining for us extra time than ever.

More time, proper right here, manner time that isn't always compulsorily taken up with the beneficial useful resource of some one of a kind sports activities however freely allotted for some goals. It manner time that may be freely invested in some thing endeavour of choice we choose.

Increased Productivity

The worst impact of stress is how it may flip that individual who changed into erstwhile powerful, who became the envy of their co-employees at paintings, who have become the characteristic model, into the final element all and sundry need to want to be.

Stress can definitely bypass us from grace to grass. You need to start making studies critiques now not really worth of even interest from a high faculty pupil regardless of the fact that you changed into a killer whale at your procedure, dominating the sphere.

Also, the electricity and time drain translate into fine one element for you: unproductivity. But when you restore strain, your glory days may want to make a comeback. How hundreds more? Any solving of pressure will move once more you in your productiveness, but the form of restore provided for in this e-book is collectively with could not most effective restore you in your beyond glory, but additionally takes you even better, allowing you to surpass your erstwhile productiveness benchmark.

Better Relationships

The malignancy and temperament that had been the made of stress have one exquisite effect on you out of a group of others: they spoil your relationships. No dating is saved from the ones consequences of strain. Your marriage, in case you are married, will very probable be the first to take the hit from amongst your relationships. You may additionally want to, if not careful, lose it for all time. Friendships also take the hit as you continue to withdraw, now not great from your partner, however additionally from pals. And in worst case conditions, you could grow to be violent in competition to them.

Living a pressure-free existence way you may get to make and hold exquisite relationships. Your marriage will no longer be headed on a collision route now not to say get dissolved. You get more time and get to plot your lifestyles to residence folks who actually rely to you. You get to spend more best time at the side of your circle of relatives, pals and cherished ones. You do now not display outward signs and symptoms of gloom now not to say drag them down your rabbit hole with you.

Actualising Goals

We all have goals in existence, whether or not or no longer such is properly or improperly described or not. With a strain-free lifestyles, you no longer simplest get greater time, cash productivity, higher relationships and so forth. You additionally get to go after your non-public goals, to make a fact of your dreams. How can you placed a smile on the face of some other at the same time as your face itself is overcast with all subjects horrible? With a thoughts such as the restore in this ebook will bestow upon you, you'll don't have any doubt in any respect as on your capability to move after and advantage your goals. Why? You have to have all it takes. You have to have the power. You will non-public the luxurious of time. You get to carry your circle of relatives alongside and on the identical time, greater may be gained from you.

CHAPTER 11: FIXING STRESS THE MINIMALIST WAY

How are you able to gain the intention of this ebook which is to lessen strain, remove anxiety and suppose positive mind the pleasant way feasible? Well, the truth is society has us burdened out to attempt too many things proper away. From childhood, we're conditioned to simply accept as actual with that the nicely really worth of a person is in his cloth possessions. We are taught to get an education in order that we becomes many stuff straight away. With this in mind, adulthood exhibits us chasing after material possessions; we're too busy obtaining and being many stuff to such a lot of human beings without delay that we grow to be forgetting to live. We are so preoccupied with being perceived as cushty and right that we grow to be getting overwhelmed below an avalanche of our own sincerely one in every of a kind doing. This is why you need to embody minimalism as a way to lowering the strain you face on a every day basis.

Minimalism at a Glance

Minimalism is a way of existence. You want to name it a philosophy, however it is not constrained to clearly thoughts. It involves now not excellent expertise and information, however moreover performing. Minimalism, as a manner of life, is aimed toward getting rid of all of the excesses of life, from the cloth to the non-cloth. What do I propose through excesses?

There is constantly a degree for enjoyable our dreams in lifestyles. Take the example of our belly. When we're hungry and then later we devour to satiate the starvation, in a few unspecified time in the future we start to sense glad. But greed, once in a while, overtakes us so that we consume extra than our frame dreams. What does the frame do to that more, that amount which profits it in no way? Of path, it passes it out.

Taking a cue then, from biology, minimalism is ready identifying the extra in all factors of our lives and removing it. Often we count on the ones 'little greater' do not rely, we expect they do now not remember however they've an impact on us in techniques not feasible.

The impact is a trickle proper right right here and there, till it becomes a pool. At this element, I may be linking the purpose here to the reasons of strain and tension.

By now, you want to don't have any objection to the truth that mind, location and time cluttering can affect our lives in the most horrible of strategies. But how do our minds, our place and our time get cluttered? Excess, Excess and greater EXCESS!!!

The thoughts can't possibly be easy. There is a degree of thoughts or thoughts to transport in. But, often instances; we fill it with more than is crucial, just as has been mentioned formerly in this ebook. How? It starts offevolved from region and time muddle i.E. Filling in our location and our time with subjects which we do now not want.

Look around your private home or your room proper now, or stable your mind decrease lower back to it in case you aren't in it right now. What do you note? A shelf of books which you have not touched in about a 12 months however that you only dirt every fortnight or weekend? What else are you capable of see? A amount of memorabilia at the centre table, objects you have got accumulated out of your travels? Let us take a tour of your take a look at. Oh, positive! There they're, all of your youngsters's books from excessive university thru university, no? In your closet are clothes, folded and placing, which have now not touched your frame in extra than six months? And in your shoe rack are shoes that you have overgrown as is with some of your clothes, and people you haven't applied in a long term.

What are all of these subjects doing in your home? Of route, you've got were given at severa times toyed with the idea of amassing together those you no longer need and giving them out to charity or promoting those ones that might despite the fact that fetch you a few bucks at a garage sale. But you've got got were given never had been given all the manner right down to it, have you ever ever? And whenever you see these gadgets, your mind goes to your want approximately them. You hate the concept of having to rummage thru your closet every morning that lets in you to determine what to place on, yet, you can't bring your self to remove the clutter.

This is exactly how space cluttering can devour into it gradual and then your mind, imparting you with problems which over time in their little selves collect into some element sincerely worrisome. But there may be more on your mind cluttering than this. How?

The society we live in now has a superb definition of happiness and achievement. These societal definitions of what happiness and fulfillment are, unluckily, are primarily based high-quality on one single fashionable: cloth ownership. Thus, our diploma of success and happiness becomes measured with the quantity of homes, the range and form of cars, the label and quantity of clothes we've were given. If you are not earning a six decide earnings with a fat bonus to healthful at the give up of the 12 months, then you definitely virtually aren't a success. If you do not have a boat or a holiday home inside the geographical location, then you definitely are not a achievement.

Like a flag to the blowing of a breeze, we find ourselves helpless in competition to these societal stereotypes. We discover ourselves actually and in reality chasing after those necessities of achievement and happiness. And due to the fact we can't have those requirements, we convince ourselves that we can not but be glad or recall ourselves a success. Or if we've got were given this stuff already, the ardent preference to keep them at the level they're and the desire to gain extra disturbs our minds. In whichever of those instructions we fall, one hassle is positive: we in no way surrender to pursue this fake happiness or even at the same time as we seem to find out it, the selection for more and more as required by means of way of society has made us now not viable to be happy.

From the simple desire to fill our area with fabric possessions, from the smooth preference to fill our time with the aid of the use of seeking to belong to the pinnacle beauty and attend greater functions and visit more places, we get ourselves actually labored up. The ensuing impact is that we in the end litter our thoughts and therefore, permit pressure and anxiety in. Eventually, we start to harbour terrible mind about ourselves, our disability and our seeming unwell success in life. How an lousy lot more can we ruin ourselves than this?

The Minimalist Mindset

Now that you are familiar with the cause of minimalism, how does minimalism definitely art work? It calls for subjects: one is adopting the minimalist thoughts-set and the opposite is acting the minimalist manner. Let us, but, attention on the first, proper here, for now.

The minimalist thoughts-set, like each unique form of mind-set, is essential to function a foundation upon which the minimalist act or pillars may be erected. The information approximately minimalism furnished inside the preceding phase are meant to assist scenario your thoughts, to make it become more receptive to minimalism. But the thoughts-set calls for greater than the initial situation. It is the attitude that permits us stay at the course even supposing it appears that naturally the going is not possible. It is the mindset that guarantees we do now not relapse right into a life of excess, one built to please a few others.

The minimalist mind is aware of that like each way of lifestyles change, it is in no manner clean at the start. But with dedication and diligence and ordinary, it will become pretty easy later. So the minimalist mind will not for motives of some essential traumatic situations surrender at the very last motive.

The minimalist mind-set is also privy to the reality that appearances are greater often than now not a façade. Appearances can be especially misleading but such deception is exactly what society's definition of happiness consists of. In the same vein, the minimalist thoughts-set does not see empty vicinity in its residence as a sign of lack as it does no longer equate wishes with needs, information the latter are what is crucial and are must-haves and the latter, the harbinger of extra. In the same line of belief, the minimalist mind isn't always afraid of getting rid of the extra in numerous factors of his life, know-how whole well that obtaining rid of such matters isn't the identical detail as wastefulness — it's far just the top notch manner to seize ones freedom from the concern, strain and tension, introduced on through society equating happiness with fabric possession and encouraging the ownership of more.

The Minimalist Way

With the minimalist attitude, strolling the minimalist way is appreciably easy, pleasurable and fun. The last effect of this is that it removes all of the sources of our problems, strain and tension. We get to stay a smooth but great life without greater and meaningless hundreds. The minimalist manner calls for two topics basically: one, figuring out what to put off; and two, getting rid of these subjects diagnosed.

- Planning

At this stage, all you're to do is apprehend that greater which eats up your bodily place, time and your highbrow location i.E. Your thoughts. How do you decide what's greater and what isn't always? A extensive kind of loose exams can be completed. How masses of those subjects do you've got? Where you have had been given more than one of these items, then put off the others and hold the most brilliant of them. Okay, you can maintain one extra, too. But why keep extra than you need? Let the stores be your warehouses and now not your own home. When end up the final time you used it? If it's miles now not whatever a whole lot much less than three months in the beyond, I am making a bet against the seeming odds that it's miles an excess which has no place in your own home. If you can not even maintain in thoughts the very last time you used it or idea approximately, the risk which you do now not want it spherical will growth.

You can preserve the diagnosed objects in a unmarried region, say a bag, and vicinity the bag at a conspicuous area in the house. If you have to visit the bag to get something greater than as quickly as in consistent with week a few of the weeks probation you are setting the contents of the bag on, then that object probable does now not need to be removed.

As you do to fabric possessions above, do equal to non-material possessions, too. Classify your relationships, as an example, into 3: primary, secondary and peripheral. Those you cannot do with out are inside the primary. Those you preserve spherical for a lesser necessity together together with your boss and partner at work fall within the 2nd category. The third is supposed for the ones whom you may do without. Do not fear; you're on a person's zero.33 elegance, too.

For the primary organization you haven't any preference but to preserve them, keep, of direction, they artwork in competition to your lifestyles. Or are you able to take away your youngsters, mother and father and associate? For the ones you could stake your self out — however make sure they'll do the equal for you, first. The 2d elegance you could maintain round. But do no longer hesitate to reduce them out if they will be the very barriers in your existence or a terrible affect. The peripheral company need not be reduce out on the drop of a coin but hold it in thoughts that people on this class need no longer serve as stressors in your existence. If for any purpose or risk, you discover them contributing to the highbrow catch 22 situation you're coping with, then, do no longer absolutely display them the door, preserve the door firmly shut

- Getting Rid of the Excess

After figuring out the ones gadgets that do not belong on your vicinity, what's subsequent? Getting rid of them! How do you do this? A style of options are available. You can convert people with sentimental rate to you to a digitised form. Why not experiment all of these photographs from the eighties and characteristic them backed up in your Google strength or OneDrive? Letters, notes and so forth may be got rid of this manner. You can also instead buy eBooks in desire to tough covers.

Why now not make a couple of bucks on the ones subjects at a garage sale? Yes, make some cash from disposing of used devices. That which you count on isn't of any value to you is of giant rate to others. Plants don't have any use for oxygen; however, you and I depend on it to stay alive.

Charity is some distinctive preference you can discover to do away with your more fabric possession. There are masses of folks that might kill for that pair of shoes of yours which you cannot even bare to test. The more garments out of your closet can go to charity, too. Help positioned a smile at the face of others. Help impart the lives of others thru giving up the more to your lives for them.

In truth, those little acts of kindness are what bring about actual happiness. The reminiscences of those linger all the time. You can relive your moments of fulfilment, which include when you helped the antique girl upstairs repair a number of her stuff. The volunteer jobs you took up, the community service you probably did of your non-public volition, and the little birthday celebration you organised to your outside for children in the neighbourhood, little Jean whom you helped on the facet of her maths venture, little Peter whom you taught a manner to resolve a quadratic equation, all of those are the real property of happiness.

- Staying a Minimalist

How do you live a minimalist? Once you have got were given the thoughts-set, it's far almost an automatic detail for you. Try it as quickly as and you'll be satisfied approximately it. You will recognize how it could put off all your issues. By freeing up bodily region for your life, thru lowering the amount of cloth possessions you depend on, you furthermore mght declutter a while and eventually your mind, that might have been concerned ill approximately these items.

To live at the minimalist course, remind your self frequently of what you stand to face or undergo in case you pick out to relapse right proper into a life in which happiness and success is dictated through manner of manner of the massive kind of your fabric possessions in place of the excellent impact you have made immediately and in a roundabout manner in the lives of others.

CHAPTER 12: Set Priorities

Wchicken commencing on the adventure to declutter your thoughts and treatment the mess indoors your head, a top notch region to begin is thru bringing some order into your life. If you normally enjoy such as you're anywhere in the palace and your thoughts is constantly in overdrive, organizing your thoughts and putting your priorities can be your salvation. Many people have a easy idea approximately what it is they need to appear in their lives and count on this is sufficient to provide them the peace of mind they lengthy for. However, the real problem lies in synergizing your numerous aspirations in a superb manner. In the primary chapter of this e-book, you'll test a few vital training at the way to set your priorities and supply every trouble of your existence the eye and time it merits. You will learn the manner to tell the distinction among urgent and critical topics and the way to cope with each based surely to your preset priorities. Finally, we are capable of wrap up the chapter with a few clean techniques that you may comply with to seamlessly categorize any and every new task that makes its way into your life. You can also want to take a few notes at the same time as reading this financial damage, so preserve a pen and paper reachable. Let's get started.

What Do You Care About?

While this can sound like a totally extensive question which you'd need to rack your thoughts that allows you to answer, it's the crucial element to information your self better and having extra manipulate over your thoughts and actions. It's drastically crucial to be honest with yourself at the same time as seeking to reply this question. There isn't any wrong or right. The entire concept is to get lower decrease back to the fundamentals to recognize who you certainly are as someone. Everybody is different, so don't try to discover your solutions via looking into specific people's lives. Instead, bypass inward and perform a bit soul-searching. Let pass of the concept that not putting your own family on the top of your priority list technique you're egocentric or self-concerned. Passing judgment on yourself is not the idea of this workout. Instead, try to act as an insignificant witness to what's going on deep down after which begin taking notes. If for any motive, you find out it hard to perceive your priorities, you can run a few "would in all likelihood you as an opportunity…?" situations. For example, ask your self, if given only a few loose hours a day, if you can alternatively spend them walking in your private commercial employer or on some notable time at the side of your own family. Analyzing your solutions, you'll be capable of exercising a realistic list of priorities that you may use to govern it gradual successfully and located your mind snug. Here are a few easy steps you could follow to create your listing of priorities:

Define Your Values

Think of your values as your very very personal code of ethics. These set you aside from all of us else and act as your north whenever you begin dropping your experience of route in existence. Self-figuring out as an honest individual who continually acts with integrity, as an instance, will assist you perceive the parameters which you get to transport interior at the same time as confronted with a sure problem or dilemma. You possibly care about giving your nice at paintings, although it sometimes way that it'll take away from it slow with your own family. This truth will permit you to draft your priorities more realistically. Whatever your values are, you need to always motive to paste to them in case you need to be true to your self and live a extra functional lifestyles.

Link Your Goals to Your Values

The subsequent step in setting your priorities is to link the values you named on your dreams and goals. You can't select a profession path that contradicts the values that you need to live thru. Make high quality that anything your thoughts is ate up with is aligned with you. Otherwise, you should drop them altogether.

Write Down Your Daily Tasks

Break down your dreams into smaller each day duties that you want to take care of. Here, you're in reality dumping your days' really worth of sports activities onto a piece of paper in case you want to rearrange, throw out, or upload greater as you be aware in shape. It doesn't want to be cohesive or targeted; you'll get to that later.

Highlight the Important Tasks

To sift via your responsibilities, you want to get lower back to the subjects which you decided are well really worth being worried about in life. Highlight all of the obligations that relate to the ones regions. For instance, in case you care about spirituality and be given as real with that it's an essential a part of your life, then highlight all the relevant sports sports that you do, like praying and meditation. Follow this same collection with all the gadgets to your listing. What do you keep high-priced in lifestyles?

Is it Urgent/Important?

One of the primary motives your thoughts is cluttered most of the time is due to the fact you fail to differentiate among urgent and vital topics. "Urgent" subjects want your immediately attention. However, they have a non-top notch effect on the big photo. Going via your emails, for instance, is pressing, irrespective of the fact that they make a contribution next to now not whatever to your actual paintings. "Important" subjects, alternatively, are generally extra lengthy-time period and feature a big impact on accomplishing your final intention. Studying, for esxample, is one of the most not unusual examples of what's essential however no longer urgent—until you have an examination the next day, that is! After having diagnosed your listing of vital responsibilities, it's now time to installation them in a manner that is inexperienced, sustainable, and smooth to maintain, without giving it lots idea. Arrange your responsibilities on every of the four quadrants of the Urgent/Important matrix.

•Urgent/Important: Tasks that make it to this quadrant obviously need your without delay hobby as they're the maximum pressing and maximum impactful.

•Urgent/Unimportant: It's endorsed which you start with obligations in this quadrant truly to get them out of the way since they want right now motion.

- Important/Non-Urgent: Tasks right right here are generally prolonged-time period desires which you'll want to carry out a hint of each day. However, they shouldn't be a motive for stress on your normal life.

- Unimportant/Non-Urgent: These are surely the obligations that you need to recognition on trimming once more or decreasing down on. They don't serve any actual cause and unnecessarily soak up location in your thoughts which you'd be better off dedicating to greater important issues.

Do a Dry Run

Now that you have a extraordinarily whole manual on a way to set your priorities, it's time to vicinity it to the check. However, before beginning, you need to manage your expectancies well an awesome manner to avoid being annoyed in case you don't get the consequences you have been hoping for. Consider it a gaining knowledge of enjoy that lets in you to set you at the right tune and prepare you to move at whole force even as you're organized. Start with what you determined are easy obligations and spot how nicely you're capable of prioritize them and organize them for every week or so. Afterward, examine your average performance and understand the disturbing conditions you confronted that didn't will will let you collect the whole benefits of this exercising.

Give Yourself the Time You Need to Make the Change

Nothing will stifle your development greater than speeding yourself into this grounded and serene version you envision. You have to understand that clearing your thoughts and retraining it in this new way of wondering and processing facts isn't always any easy feat. It will take masses of time and effort in advance than you begin seeing any actual alternate. However, the key's to pat yourself at the returned on every occasion you manipulate to banish thoughts that don't serve you and undeservingly eat location for your mind. Remind your self that even the slightest improvement is considered a win. Moreover, this can encourage you to hold going, to in the long run advantage the dominion of thoughts which you are aiming for.

Finalize Your List and Have it "Laminated"

Once you've got got got completed collectively along with your list of priorities, recognize that even as the content material fabric will change with time, the layout, if we will name it that, will continuously live the equal. Having this sorted out will assist a extraordinary cope with clearing your thoughts, as you'll have a preset shape to conform with with any new challenge that arises in the future. You'll discover your self mechanically reading and categorizing at the same time as not having to provide it lots belief.

This technique is all approximately going head-first into the mess and digging via the masses of thoughts which can be on foot thru your mind at any given time. You want to apprehend that matters can also get worse in advance than they get better, however you may be able to advantage the peaceful nation of thoughts you wish for if you maintain this sample in thoughts. Only then will you be capable of kiss your issues good-bye and make way for happiness and abundance on your life.

In the following bankruptcy, you'll observe the significance of constructing a strong ordinary to help relieve your anxieties and stay a happier lifestyles.

Chapter 13: Develop a Routine

Amessy mind is disruptive. That's why it's crucial for every one humans to make room for recuperation via clean every day changes. Although the idea of making a regular can sound absurd to a person suffering to take control of their life, developing a every day routine is the important thing to feeling extra on top of factors and prioritizing your highbrow fitness. Routines help you installation healthy behavior, cope with alternate, and decrease pressure degrees. Start your every day recurring with an anti-strain morning practice because healthful morning conduct set the tone for the rest of the day. Routines are known to significantly help with anxiety and melancholy. If you bewith the aid of any of those highbrow troubles, you'll phrase a big difference for your mood and each day conduct, similarly to many exquisite super benefits that accompany a wholesome day by day everyday. It surely is a very beneficial technique to apply for your every day life if you're attempting to find to declutter your thoughts and stay pressure-loose. So, how are you going to increase a every day regular, and the way appropriate is this approach to your highbrow fitness? This bankruptcy talks approximately the severa advantages of following a each day strain-unfastened ordinary and lists some pointers that will help you come up with yours.

The Mental Benefits of Having a Routine

Daily workouts are not quite lots that sweet feeling of accomplishment on the surrender of the day. They are also a exceptional manner for plenty human beings to prioritize highbrow and bodily health. Every preference we make consumes some of our mind's strength of will reserves. Unfortunately, a few studies aspect inside the path of the electricity of mind of the mind as being a confined beneficial aid, meaning that you steadily lose your capability to show down brief gratification as you flow into through your day. By automating your morning behavior, you narrow out a few strength of will-depleting sports activities, which consist of locating out whether or not to turn off your alarm clock or now not. Let's speak exclusive strain-preventing benefits of growing a every day routine.

Anchor Effects

Routine works wonders on making us revel in anchored, irrespective of what we go through in our day. There's actual comfort in knowing that you're however going to have your 6 pm meal or which you're notwithstanding the reality that going to get to visit mattress at 10 pm together with you constantly do. Life is complete of uncertainties, which motives lots of us to sense stressful for no purpose. However, the expertise of a ordinary combats that feeling and allows you sense more settled and anchored internally. It may be plenty much less difficult to deal with surprising time periods when you have your very very own each day shape in area.

Stress Management

Having a to-do listing and looking to do not forget topics off your listing may be overwhelming to hold on a daily foundation. It's an entire lot of strain seeking to control the whole thing taking area to your day. A ordinary lets you cement masses of your each day activities so you don't need to take into account them anymore. You simply do them as part of your computerized agenda. This can be seen in the example of brushing your teeth every day. You don't need to assume or pressure about brushing your enamel. You just automatically do it after breakfast. When uncertainties and stressful alternatives are eliminated from your day, you get to experience extra in control of your lifestyles.

Making Time for Priorities

Having a every day primarily based ordinary allows you to locate time for the topics which may be actually important to you. We all want time to have amusing, loosen up, or virtually play with a puppy. This can be without troubles squeezed into your every day time table if you manipulate to make bigger an prepared ordinary. Of direction, there will normally be instances at the same time as someone all at once pops in or even as artwork takes three instances so long as you deliberate for, however you'll manage to address the ones conditions even as you consist of downtime on your each day workout. Structuring your day will will allow you to revel in best time, along with spending greater time together together along with your children, taking emotional pauses, and having extra time typically to prioritize yourself and your desires.

Cultivating Positive Daily Habits

Having a structured ordinary in vicinity permits you nurture terrific conduct and pay greater interest to self-care. When you arrange a while, you control to designate certain time blocks for hobbies and sports that you wouldn't normally have time for. This consists of making your very very own breakfast, making your mattress, or perhaps workout. Routines are tremendous for liberating up more time and let you preserve music of your every day sports activities. They gift an super possibility so that you can embody as many quality behavior as you may for your day.

Exercising

Although exercising isn't all and sundry's cup of tea, it's a outstanding way to relieve strain and lift your temper. There are many clinical research and statistics that again up the first-rate effect of exercise on an individual's temper and self esteem. However, maximum people discover it hard to suit an workout regular into their day by day schedules. This in which a balanced each day routine is to be had in reachable. When you have were given an organized every day plan, you can effects make time for workout. This will help you experience performed and green and help in decluttering your mind. Even if you could handiest healthy a couple of exercising schooling into your week, you may nevertheless enjoy that identical feeling of accomplishment.

How to Develop a Routine

Now that we've established what a healthy every day routine is and why it's unique in your intellectual health, it's time to dig into how you may observe this to your each day existence.

Start through Making Your Bed

You might imagine making your mattress is a chore. Well, it's far, besides it can additionally make you feel right about your self. That's our aim right right here. Helping you declutter your mind thru decluttering your vicinity. It can also sound ironic, but a cluttered area contributes to a messy thoughts and a annoying lifestyles. However, making your mattress can art work some psychological magic for your mood and behavior as nicely. By wearing out the first venture of the day, you get a revel in of success that drives you to begin and stop other obligations. It takes time to exercise this approach, especially on the same time as everyone have a take a look at it as a similarly useless chore, but who wouldn't need to move slowly proper proper right into a clean, tidy mattress after a protracted day?

Organize Your "Getting Ready" Routine

It's vital to phrase that the extra your intellectual fitness improves, the greater picks you've got on autopilot, and the much less complicated your life becomes. It moreover gives you better manipulate over your selections. You don't need to turn out to be with a case of choice fatigue on the quit of the day. Routine permits you arrange those morning sports activities activities collectively with brushing your teeth, doing all your hair, and getting dressed. This way, you keep away from stressful your self over what to do next. To installation a healthy regular, start together with your morning conduct. Your morning regular ought to consist of prepared and automatic micro-options that don't absorb plenty of your mental vicinity. Organize the early morning sports that assist you get organized so that it will begin your day with a glowing begin.

Add Deep Breathing Breaks to Your Schedule

Taking deep breaths works immediately to drop your anxiety levels and calm you down. It at once lowers the cortisol degrees in your frame, it truly is the hormone responsible for strain. Taking deep breaths is one of the awesome pressure-relieving answers ever. You want to encompass breathing breaks into your each day schedule and observe how this affects your mood and conduct. Set a timer and take a break each hour orto take deep breaths and adjust your feelings of anxiety.

Do Frequent Emotional Checks

The reality is that we stay in a less than wonderful worldwide wherein topics go incorrect all of the time. You can't forestall yourself from getting angry each time topics don't pass the manner you need them to, but you may teach your self to let go and get maintain of the worst conditions. Make time to sit down down through yourself and ponder the topics which could have bothered or burdened you out within the path of your day. It's k to have terrible feelings within the path of amazing every day events, but you need to deal with them on the give up of the day and make certain you easy out any judgments you preserve toward them. This will assist you sleep better at night time time and sense greater on top of factors of your feelings. By taking time to test up for your feelings, you can manipulate to release poor judgments and get rid of any underlying tension.

Sleep Routine

Having an prepared everyday allows you to sleep at constant instances, get sufficient hours of sleep, and wake up at the same time each day regular together along with your plan. When you put together some time, you get to have some more time for yourself to wind down earlier than going to mattress. This may be truly powerful in coping with insomnia and could assist you sleep better at night time. When you prepare your day by day routine, make sure you cope with your sleeping sample and take note of how many hours of sleep you get in keeping with night time time. A accurate quantity of sleep to live healthy is round 7-eight hours at the least. Lack of sleep equals loss of manipulate over feelings, pressure, anxiety, and lots of others., and in the long run lack of a clear mind. Sleep is vital!

Routines are designed to help people advantage more manage over their every day conduct. They help us live prepared and facilitate our each day obligations thru the usage of automating most of our not unusual picks. Your thoughts holds a constrained quantity of place for choices and electricity of will, because of this that the greater picks you burden yourself with, the a good buy an awful lot much less you'll be able to make right alternatives in a while for your day. You need to take gain of your thoughts's ability through releasing up extra region for self-care. That's why exercising routines are the remarkable with reference to prioritizing your mental fitness and eliminating stress.

Chapter 14: Journaling

As you start to create a ordinary, one of the maximum critical things which you need to do is determine out a way to externalize your thoughts, so that you don't experience like your thoughts is constantly scrolling through to-do gadgets and random topics which can have come to you at a few degree inside the day.

The exquisite way to do that? Consider starting a mag.

Journaling now not most effective allows you get your mind out on paper but also gives you the time and location to analyze and prepare those thoughts. Additionally, journals are generally small enough to be portable – because of this that that in case you ever start to experience crushed at some point of the day, it's smooth to write a few notes in your journal earlier than returning to some thing you have been doing.

There's no one right way to start journaling – it's all about what works satisfactory for you and the manner elaborate you want to be. No rely which approach you select, journaling is an effective way to declutter your thoughts.

Research posted within the American Psychological Association's Journal of Experimental Psychology noted that expressive writing, or the exercise of placing your mind and feelings on paper, can assist enhance your running reminiscence and remove non-prevent and intrusive mind you can have about awful occasions you've got got skilled.

This, in flip, enables unfastened up your mind and lets in you to dedicate more assets to more vital highbrow sports, at the side of dealing with stress. A record from the University of Rochester Medical Center notes that journaling every day will have a plethora of highbrow fitness blessings, together with managing anxiety and despair.

How to Start Journaling

If you've never journaled earlier than, starting this addiction can appear intimidating. Not great do you want to teach yourself to be cushty with writing out your mind and feelings, however there's additionally the question of methods you must begin, what magazine you should buy, and what journaling method you want to apply.

There's no wrong fashion with journaling – if it's some detail that works for you and that makes you revel in better, then it's the proper way of doing it. Similarly, there's no person brand of magazine you should purchase to start journaling – you could even begin on free sheets of paper and bind them collectively to create a magazine if you have the time!

That stated, in case you're now not positive of in which to begin, there are various techniques of journaling you may check with. Let's test some of the ones.

Free Writing

Getting started out as a loose writer is straightforward – all you want to do is prepared a timer, pull up your magazine and pen, and start writing. Then write at some point of the timer, letting your thoughts and feelings float onto the net web page with out preventing to think.

If you may't set a time restrict, set an internet web web page restriction – this is, what number of pages you want to write down each free-writing session. When journaling the usage of this method, you shouldn't stop to edit what you wrote or write in best sentences. Instead, write something comes to your thoughts. If you find out yourself going for walks out of thoughts which you want to get out onto the web page, don't fear – write some aspect comes on your mind next, whether or not that's your grocery listing or a contemporary concept for paintings.

Getting those thoughts onto paper allows you to connect to your sincere, uncensored self. It facilitates you grow to be extra accepting of your thoughts and feelings in place of permitting them to percolate to your mind and reason anxiety.

The power of unfastened-writing lies in its capacity that will help you get in touch in conjunction with your proper self without demanding approximately how distinctive humans will select you or how proper you sound to the sector. While the concept of putting a timer may additionally additionally appear intimidating, it doesn't should be for lengthy – even 5-10 mins each day will assist.

Bullet Journal

If you've looked at human beings posting photographs in their journals online, you've possibly encountered this approach earlier than. Highly famous, it changed into evolved via Ryder Carroll, a digital fashion style clothier who to start with used it as a way to manipulate his ADHD.

A bullet mag now not handiest permits you propose your day but additionally lets in you replicate on your movements and emotions. These journals include a hint of the whole thing, from to-do lists and schedules to brainstorming mind, reminders, notes, and greater.

A appreciably extra prepared method of journaling than freewriting, it lets in you to set up your thoughts. You may have a have a look at the notes and to-do lists you've made and take the critical steps to make sure that they're finished and no longer cluttering your mind. Additionally, this method permits you apprehend what components of your lists are most important to you, as you've got the whole lot written down, and people can be outcomes analyzed.

Bullet journaling has come to be so famous that many stationery corporations now promote committed bullet journals, making it as smooth as feasible to begin one yourself. Alternatively, you could look at the diverse flat lays published on social media to function your idea.

Reading Journal

Are you an avid reader? Do you discover yourself forgetting vital plot facts in books you look at and loved, forcing you to re-examine the same pages over and over all over again?

If so, a analyzing magazine is a high-quality answer.

This kind of journaling permits you to get the most out of the media you consume, whether or now not that be books or articles. You can also even amplify it to cowl movies, tv suggests, and podcasts.

Through a studying magazine, you can track the books you've observe, make a word of the most essential plot factors and characters, and report charges and passages that you cherished. With these thoughts out on paper, they won't clutter your mind – and the following time you're wondering what passed off in your favored ebook, you can honestly refer again to your magazine in preference to re-analyzing it!

A reading mag can also are to be had in on hand for university students – this fashion of journaling lets in you to make notes approximately the books you take a look at, have a take a look at them, and reflect at the information you've fed on. You can even record observations or particular facts you take a look at in a ebook and would love to make a word of, making it super for non-fiction and educational books in addition to fictional ones.

No matter which fashion of journaling you choose, it's critical to ensure you permit yourself time and location to reflect. It's now not enough to truly get your mind on paper – you need to keep in thoughts the effect that having those thoughts crowded to your thoughts is having on you. Think approximately whether or not or now not you're willing to permit flow of them, and hold in mind the top notch way to lessen the danger of feeling overwhelmed on your private mind over again.

Chapter 15: Allow Time to Reflect

Self-reflected picture is one of the exquisite ways to declutter your mind. It permits you to mentally disconnect from the physical worldwide and lets in relieve strain and anxiety while providing mental clarity. However, self-mirrored picture isn't an smooth technique to understand and calls for you to broaden the functionality to cognizance. It is not a way that you can practice just as quick as and witness improvements. It ought to be advanced and built right into a addiction. Once mastered, it offers you the functionality to be privy to your self, an hobby that operates no longer simply mentally however additionally physical, emotionally, religiously, and spiritually.

Decluttering your thoughts will permit you to benefit reputation and increase your productivity. Self-mirrored image is a incredible manner of accomplishing a pointy usa of thoughts. This monetary destroy will guide you on the manner to apply self-mirrored picture to your gain. What Is Self-Reflection?

Self-reflected picture is each specific manner of describing meditation. It is the exercise of letting pass of all random mind, freeing your past, now not fretting about your destiny, and searching into your self, your feelings, emotions, conduct, and beliefs.

Self-contemplated image is like searching at your self in a replicate, except this reflected image isn't always pores and pores and skin deep. You don't sincerely have a study your self, but indoors your self to assess your thoughts and movements, your individual and man or woman, what motivates you and what holds you lower once more. It is about facts your goals and facts the motives at the back of them.

Self-contemplated photograph can display very beneficial. It let you distance yourself from all of the distractions in life to recognition completely on you. It helps you to take a look at the larger photo however with out missing out at the minor info. It lets you recognize in that you are heading, your trajectory in existence. You will have a have a look at whether or not or no longer your thoughts are everyday with your desires or whether you need to make some adjustments. The paintings of self-reflected photograph does no longer come with out issues, although. Letting go of all the distractions in your existence, the thoughts that hassle you, the horrible emotions that mess around in an limitless circle on your thoughts, and focusing for your inner self requires exercising and electricity of thoughts. To virtually revel in the benefits of self-reflected photograph, it wishes to be practiced every day. So, you must take the time from your busy time table to permit your self to self-mirror.

Benefits of Self Reflection

Self-mirrored photo calls for dedicating some time every day to in truth popularity to your thoughts and feelings and recognize your inner-being. You can be thinking if it's important enough to be able to take time out of your busy time table to determine to this hobby. The brief and sweet solution is, "Yes!" Here are some of the blessings of self-mirrored photo that have to persuade you of its significance and provide an purpose of why it deserves a niche to your daily time desk.

Make Sense of Chaos

One of the advantages of self-mirrored image is that it lets you make experience out of chaos. It allows you order your thoughts, emotions, and feelings. Focusing at the multitude of thoughts that keep floating spherical to your head will let you installation them, recognize them higher, apprehend their belongings, and decrease frustration and confusion. This, in turn, allows you benefit mental clarity and enhance your capacity to popularity. This is exactly what decluttering your mind is ready.

Track Your Progress and Understand Your Trajectory

Self-mirrored photograph lets in you apprehend what drives you and what motivates you. It permits you recognize in which you're heading and if this is the path that you want to move. It helps you to look once more for your past and research from your errors. It furthermore enables you realize how your existence has modified over time and the manner you would really like it to exchange inside the future. It lets you leave in the returned of materialistic attachments and consciousness on matters that certainly rely to you.

Road to Self-Awareness

Self-focus is fundamental to real happiness. However, it's far safe to mention that no person is aware of you higher than your self. It is more than probable which you don't honestly understand yourself further to you discovered you do. Self-refection can help exchange that. Self-recognition comes through connecting collectively together along with your internal emotions and your internal demons. Understanding what bothers you and restrains your functionality is without a doubt as vital as data what drives you and motivates you to maintain going. Understanding your self results in contentment and happiness. It furthermore permits you to mention no to the topics that are not in alignment with you.

Boost Your Confidence

Self-mirrored image allows you conquer your fears. It may be very commonplace for humans to doubt their competencies. This fear can frequently be rooted in failures out of your past. By helping you gain self notion on your functionality, self-mirrored image ought to have a proper away effect in your outlook on existence and your personal and expert achievement. This is as it offers you the courage to tackle possibilities which you may not have otherwise taken into consideration your self particular sufficient for.

Look at the Bigger Picture

Self-mirrored image enables you learn how to forget about approximately the trivial matters in life and not live upon them. It allows you recognize that bygones are bygones. It gives you the ability to have a have a have a look at the bigger photograph, interest, and artwork in the direction of the topics that during reality remember to you.

What Should You Reflect On?

While practising self-reflected picture, there are numerous topics which you need to invite your self. The purpose of self-mirrored image is to discover the solutions to the ones questions. Here are some questions that you want to be asking:

- What are your strengths?

- What have you ever ever completed over the years, and what do you simply desire to attain?

- What challenges do you face? How a lot of those traumatic conditions are self-imposed and self-created?

- What makes you happy? What are the moments you cherish the most and the moments that offer you with emotional contentment?

- What are your weaknesses? Can any of your weaknesses be have become benefits?

- What are the main troubles on your existence? What are the answers to the ones problems?

- What bothers you the most? Do the topics that problem you clearly have an effect on you in your each day existence? Can you do something high-quality about it, or are they beyond your manipulate?

Self-mirrored image can be your tool for self-discovery and inner peace. It will let you discover your stressful situations and overcome them. At the identical time, it will let you understand your biggest strengths and weaknesses and artwork on them. Self-reflection ought to be superior as a addiction. It must be threaded into your manner of existence. The advantages of self-contemplated picture are proper now obvious, however quite some humans commonly tend to give up after just a few days of attempting. Once you get past that preliminary level, despite the truth that, you will be able to test a huge development for your normal existence in terms of pressure, anxiety, clarity of mind, and your capacity to attention. The extremely good way of doing this is to commit a difficult and speedy time of the day to exercise self-mirrored image. Early in the morning is probably the tremendous time to obtain this and could provide the exquisite consequences, however you are unfastened to exercise self-contemplated photo each time it's far convenient for you.

Chapter 16: Let Go of the Past

Past and former trauma may be a heavy burden to carry to your shoulders, specially at the equal time as you refuse to allow skip of your past. The problem is, at the same time as you hold on to the past, it prevents you from progressing and living within the moment. You acquired't be able to become who you actually need to be. This is due to the truth we will be predisposed to create troubles in order that we are capable of deliver ourselves a feel of identity. Chasing this experience of identification exposes us to our painful beyond reports and stops us from residing within the present. We grow to be so connected to our struggles due to the truth we don't realise what our lives could be like with out them. This is why letting go can be significantly tough. Imagine letting skip of your faux ideals, horrible studies, unhealthy relationships, and terrible conduct. These matters generally reason fear and fear, which take over your mind in the future and shape your movements. However, this prevents us from seeing the splendor of the moment. That being said, anybody have our past struggles, however they don't outline who we are. Only you may define who you're and what you want to be. Let's test how you can take a stand and allow flow of your beyond.

Why You Should Let Go of Your Past

When you preserve directly to the past and ruminate on preceding possibilities that might have befell, you get stuck in an terrible usa of thoughts replaying the guilt, damage, and shame over and over another time. You obsess about the matters that you anticipated to appear, the emotions you could't allow pass of or the people who didn't love you in the identical way that you loved them, and the difficult relationships that challenged your fitness and integrity. While letting pass of these things may be the maximum hard element you ever needed to do, it's far truely certainly one in all your most effective paths to growth. Here's why you may't maintain on in your past struggles and why you need to permit pass of the past in advance than it begins shaping your actions in the present.

The Past Cannot Be Changed

No endure in thoughts how an entire lot electricity, time, or feelings you spend money on looking to trade the past, you could in no way change the information. You can't alternate what passed off, but you can trade the manner you react to it. So, in choice to letting beyond disappointments and struggles form your moves, you can direct your emotions and thoughts to a more fine path so that you can examine instructions and understanding from those poor conditions. Think of yourself as a non-forestall work in progress and understand that your struggles are truly there to help you increase your person. The greater you expand, the more you discover ways to look another time at beyond encounters as stepping stones main to your destiny self.

Your Past Does Not Define You

Your past can be a part of your records, however it's not who you're. The previous reviews may also make up a part of your character, but the manner they represent themselves relies upon honestly on you. You can leave your very personal imprint at the way conditions take region and take manage of the way you allow them to form you. You certainly want to remember that your identity is as a whole lot part of your destiny as it is your beyond. So, you need to save you your moves from getting impacted with the useful resource of beyond activities. When you sink down into your preceding trauma, you pass over out on residing within the present or dwelling to your tomorrow.

You Manage to Make Space for Something New

Holding on to your beyond is like having a closet complete of vintage junk that you not need. Most of the time, this antique junk handiest slows you down and takes up quite a few your intellectual area. That's why you need to pause and preserve on great to the matters which you actually need as a way to improvement. We're talking about the assets you bodily, spiritually, psychologically, and emotionally need. Ask your self, do the identical matters I maintain onto make experience as they did once more at that factor of my life? Why am I afraid to permit them to bypass? Is it a case of nostalgia for the beyond, or am I actually afraid to miss approximately those painful activities? When you smooth out those intellectual demons keeping you once more, you're making area to your mind for logo spanking new subjects to appear.

You Become Stronger

Letting float of the past, antique conduct, struggles, and those who aren't accurate for you is sincerely a hard task. That's why many choose to live exactly in which they're. They refuse to get out in their consolation vicinity. Everyone could have an excuse as to why they obtained't permit pass of their beyond. However, letting skip requires pretty some emotional energy and staying energy. It makes you more potent and more strong. Letting skip lets in you to stay inside the 2nd and recognition on who you clearly want to turn out to be. That's why humans with emotional electricity and adulthood endure in thoughts themselves nearly invincible.

How to Let Go of the Past

While letting skip of the past permits you're making a big change on your existence, it additionally substantially improves your health. When you get stuck on your beyond struggles and maintain ruminating about the things which you predicted to arise, your frame enters a fight-or-flight nation, that could eventually harm your fitness. Anxiety reasons a number of health conditions, which includes gastroesophageal reflux and heart attacks because of expanded blood pressure. When you figure on letting flow of your past and freeing your thoughts of that vain strain, the health benefits start performing proper away. So, how can you workout letting flow of the past? Here are the number one steps.

Build Physical Distance

We frequently concentrate someone advise staying an extended way from the individual or scenario that delivered on us to be disillusioned. That's truly very beneficial to deal with traumatic conditions or to avoid stress in trendy. What this indicates is that in case you take the time a long way from a situation or man or woman causing you strain, you received't ought to take into account it or stay reminded of it as a good buy. This in the long run allows you flow on and allow bypass. Not having to technique the scenario all of the time facilitates you easy your thoughts and permit flow into of painful triggers that could remind you of annoying thoughts. It is constantly much less hard to distance your self from the state of affairs. Both physical and intellectual distance is wanted in the ones conditions. You need to offer your thoughts a damage from continuously having to think about a painful event.

Turn Off Your Fight or Flight Response

Most of our confusion, stress, and emotions of being overwhelmed are firmly installation thru worry. Fear controls loads of our risky alternatives, and this places your body in a everyday combat-or-flight mode. We don't commonly sit down down right right down to ask ourselves why we're genuinely disenchanted or irritated. You want to write down down your triggers and find out the motives of your fear. Create a self-care mantra in that you remind yourself of why you maintain going or the way to stay grounded. Ask yourself, are the ones issues in fact real? Are you surely a awful mother without a doubt because you had one orterrible days? When you deal with situations to your non-public, it allows you benefit self assure, and also you don't need to be in a combat-or-flight mode all the time.

Practice Mindfulness

Mindfulness is all approximately being present inside the 2nd. By dwelling in the present, we avoid having mind of our past or destiny affect our present picks. When you convey your consciousness onto the prevailing, you advantage more freedom, prevent your beyond harm from attending to you, and pick the way you need to stay your existence. This is why it's vital that you start training mindfulness to help together along side your aim of letting flow of the beyond.

Don't Be Hard on Yourself

Usually, our first reaction to failure is self-grievance. Sometimes, you can't be capable of permit bypass, but you need to cope with your self like you'll treat a chum and forgive your self for now not having the functionality to accomplish some of your desires. Pain is inevitable, and there's no way you can forestall it from happening, however you may trade the manner you respond to it and take it clean on yourself while matters don't circulate as deliberate. Show your self a few kindness and compassion as you'll do with a pal, and also you'll be capable of make better picks and eliminate guilt.

Address Your Triggers and Allow Them to Happen

We all normally generally tend to cover or strive to break out from our horrible feelings. Feelings like unhappiness, anger, grief, and disappointment can seem so tough to cope with that we hide them away to avoid them. What that does is prevents us from letting flow and transferring on. Instead, you need to cope with your poor feelings and allow your feelings go with the float a good way to cope with the scenario in a wholesome manner. Otherwise, you can sincerely emerge as caught inside the beyond and no longer capable of shipping on. Identify your triggers and embody their impact to your mentality so that you can manipulate them within the destiny and allow cross of your past.

Letting drift of the beyond may be a sensitive topic for masses of us. The purpose for this is because we want to keep a number of our sense of identity. We assume that the ones horrible emotions and former events make up who we are. The reality is, your past does now not outline you, and you're able to doing extra than you can have anticipated in reality through the usage of manner of releasing your thoughts from those useless burdens and specializing within the present.

Chapter 17: Schedule a Digital Break

In nowadays's global, we are able to see digital devices in every nook of our lives, and it's nearly inconceivable to live without them. Everything from our paintings to our social lives relies upon on those gadgets. We ought to have a look at paintings-associated emails, memos, assembly reminders, and masses of different subjects on our gadgets. We even ought to depend on immediately messaging and social media apps to speak with our buddies and own family.

Due to the cutting-edge pandemic and the following lockdowns, the arena came to a standstill and had it no longer been for those virtual gadgets, the global monetary system would possibly have collapsed. However, it additionally meant an expanded dependence on those devices to stay associated with the rest of the arena.

Most folks already pick out textual content messages and voice calls over meeting in individual. Many humans have even related the use of technology with entertainment—it truly is a volatile manner of questioning.

When we have not anything else to do, we turn towards our mobiles and laptop structures to entertain us. The a couple of streaming apps, video video video games, video content material cloth, and one-of-a-kind structures maintain us entertained for hours on stop.

However, we have have been given one choice to cope with this addiction, and this is boycotting those devices. Now, this doesn't mean that you need to % your stuff up and head over to the Himalayas to live lifestyles like an ascetic. This truly method that you take a brief damage from indulgence in those gadgets every on occasion.

We can't stand a single second with out our cellular telephones or internet connectivity. If we ever must face the ones situations, then we experience awkward and pressured, as if some factor is missing from our lives. This dependence isn't a superb trouble and isn't any precise from an addiction a person can increase for opiates or alcohol. A brief damage will make certain which you expand strength of will and reticence to address the urge within the destiny.

How to Take a Break?

If you're thinking how you may take this so-known as virtual break to give up the cycle of dependence on your digital gadgets, then don't fear. This phase will discover the one of a type steps you could take to make certain you stay impartial of these devices.

However, it'll take some of effort and strength of will on your element. Even despite the fact that those strategies are very sluggish, you could find it hard to forestall using your devices because of your dedication to staying cautiously in touch with human beings. It can be hard before the whole thing, but it slowly receives lots less complex and much less complicated. With sufficient exercise, you'll be a strength of thoughts guru in no time.

Know Your Purpose

Whenever you're on line, don't just wander away inside the infinite waves of content material. It's very clean to get engrossed in a few factor that you didn't even intend to do within the first place. If you can hold in thoughts what you opened your tool for, you can manage your subsequent movements to a first rate quantity. You can try to make a to-do listing of all the topics which you choice to perform earlier than you get proper of access on your device honestly so it's less complex to stay heading inside the right route.

Suppose you need to complete some place of job paintings, have a few duties coated up earlier of time. You have to prioritize each project and make a list so you can strike off every one after it's miles been completed. An instance of this listing is given beneath. You can use this as a model for your list to make your workflow greater targeted and prepared.

1. Research problem depend "ABC."

2. Write a record on the scenario "ABC."

three. Mail the record to the clients.

4. Finish writing the every day paintings report.

five. Finalize the day's duties.

Put Away Your Devices

This advice sounds a good deal less hard than it virtually is. All you want to do is placed your gadgets somewhere you can't without troubles get right of entry to them. However, imposing this tip might be the most hard a part of a digital ruin. You want to make sure that the location you're placing your gadgets in isn't effects available. If you could with out problem attain out to seize your tool, then it's as a substitute probable that you'll destroy your decision.

One properly concept is probably to fasten those gadgets away in a drawer or a cabinet and give up the keys to someone you consider. Your achievement will depend on whether or no longer or now not this individual entails a selection at hand over the important trouble to you or not, so pick out wisely. As a long way as cellular phones are concerned, you could still need to acquire vital calls. To maintain using your mobile smartphone normally, you could strive switching to a characteristic telephone in choice to a telephone. The function phones are basically telephones ready with number one features like textual content messaging and calling. These devices are to be had at dirt-cheap charges and may be a excellent manner to substitute appreciably distracting smartphones.

Quit Social Media

Social media may be taken into consideration considered one of the maximum crucial distractions you face each day. The worst part approximately social media dependancy is that it's no longer your fault, every. Social media apps are designed to hold human beings stuck to them always. Companies spend masses of lots of dollars studying new methods to make their feed greater attractive to clients. The endless barrage of stories and posts on Instagram or the each day updates of your Facebook friends can be too tempting to stop. You can simply keep scrolling endlessly without ever seeing the ultimate of it, and this wastes loads of your valuable time.

Uninstalling the ones apps or—in case you experience a touch extreme—deleting your bills on the ones systems can be a brilliant way to reduce your virtual dependancy. Once those apps are lengthy gone and your device is going for walks best the maximum essential apps, you may popularity at the crucial subjects in a miles better way. This can be an super alternative for disposing of your cell telephone as this can be an extended-term answer in region of a brief-term one.

Negative Effects of Digital Dependence

We now understand the excellent processes you can reduce your dependence on virtual gadgets. However, you still need to recognize why you want to make the leap, and that is because of the truth there are numerous risky outcomes of virtual dependence. Once you're aware about the ones horrible outcomes, you'll locate it lots much less complicated to give up this dependancy for correct.

Depression and Anxiety

The heavy customers of social media frequently find themselves cut off from the relaxation of the area. These humans rely almost certainly on those systems to have any kind of social interplay, and that they regularly discover themselves without any actual-international buddies when they need actual resource. While social media could have a great impact on the mind-set of a person if all in their interactions on-line are great, this is not usually the case. The maximum not unusual form of interplay everybody has online is awful.

People on social media say and do topics that they wouldn't say or do in real life. This independence to do anything one pleases can reason misuse of these liberties and toxic conduct. Most people come across this shape of conduct online, which could cause depression. Additionally, humans regularly get nerve-racking once they see someone they recognise acting a good deal better in lifestyles than they may be. This might not be actual at all because of the truth that people need to project a pretentious picture on social media. However, it may motive comparisons and feelings of guilt or of being left behind, which can also motive despair often.

www.ingramcontent.com/pod-product-compliance
Lightning Source LLC
Chambersburg PA
CBHW050402120526
44590CB00015B/1794